SUSAN QUILLIAM

love
coach

No one's ever shown you how to make love work.
Until now.

Thorsons

Thorsons
An Imprint of HarperCollins*Publishers*
77–85 Fulham Palace Road,
Hammersmith, London W6 8JB

The Thorsons website address is: www.thorsons.com

Published by Thorsons 2000

1 3 5 7 9 10 8 6 4 2

Text illustration by Francesca Cassavetti

A catalogue record for this book
is available from the British Library

ISBN 0 7225 3986 X

Printed and bound in Great Britain by
Caledonian International Book Manufacturing Ltd, Glasgow

Acknowledgements

This book could never have been written without the expertise and experiences of many individuals and couples that I've known and worked with professionally and personally over the years.

So I'd like to thank both those who have chosen not to be named, and the following colleagues and friends: Barry; Richard Broome; Julia Cole, couple counsellor and psychosexual therapist; Anna Dalton, life skills coach; Barbara Grote; Jean Mann, hypnotherapist and member of the British Institute of Hypnotherapists; Paul and Linda McCartney and Jeff Baker; John Seymour of John Seymour Associates, Professional NLP Training; Corinne Sweet, writer, broadcaster, counsellor and agony aunt for Top Santé magazine; Erica Wagner; Willem and Jane Warren Mulder; and everyone in The Chalkface Project office, especially Miranda Broadhurst.

I'd also like to give special thanks to Barbara Levy, my agent, for her continuing expertise and support.

To my assistants June Bulley, Suzy Faithfull, Nicola Renson and Michelle Woolley for their loyalty, support and administrative excellence. And to everyone at Thorsons for commissioning and backing this book, especially Wanda, Lizzy, Hatty and Megan.

NB: This isn't the book for you if your relationship is in crisis, or if you and your partner can never feel good about each other or cooperate with each other. If so, turn to the final section of this book for details of the sort of support you need.

To Ian, who makes all things possible – even love.

Contents

Read this before you read on

They looked as if they'd been born in love.

John and Claire were old friends of my parents. And the whole time I knew them, as I was growing up, they seemed to be completely happy together.

They laughed at each other's jokes. They finished each other's sentences. They'd supported each other through his bankruptcy and her illness – and the death of one of their children.

And still, after so many years together, if one of them spoke, the other looked across and really, really listened.

I got to know John and Claire better when I reached my early twenties. My mother was dying and they were part of the brigade who ferried me backwards and forwards from the hospital. Time after time I'd walk tearfully back to their car across the hospital car park, and they'd be sitting there in the front seat, side by side, each reading a book. Still as much in love as ever.

Or so it seemed.

And then my mother died. At the funeral, totally dazed, I found myself sitting next to Claire. We talked about how my father was coping, and I said I supposed that when someone dies, their partner is always devastated. She looked at me sideways, and then said, 'I wouldn't have been, when we were first married'.

I gulped. What do you say when someone casually slips it in that their relationship hasn't always been perfect? But I wanted to know the story. And she wanted to tell me. So she told me: How when they got married and starting living together, they were head over heels in love. But how pretty soon, she'd started crying herself to sleep. How their rows used to wake the neighbours most nights for the first year. How sex had disappeared almost completely for another eighteen months. And how they'd shrieked 'divorce' at each other regularly – even though it wasn't even really possible in those days.

But slowly, things got better. It stopped hurting for whole weeks at a time. The rows tailed off, and the talking got more frequent. They found themselves making love again. Until they'd reached the relationship that I'd seen. Born in love.

But how? I asked. How had the change happened? Claire said, 'At the beginning we wanted each other – but we didn't actually love each other. It's been hard, and still is hard a lot of the time. But over the years, we've just ... learned how to love.'

I have to say it made sense to me immediately. Yes, 'learning how to love' goes against everything we hear nowadays – about how love's an instant explosion of feeling that automatically carries you through to a happy-ever-after ending. But actually, it's not like that at all.

Because personally, though my life's been full of great relationships – culminating in a wonderful marriage – it's often been a struggle. To balance out what I want and what my partner wants. To do the giving as well as the taking. To keep loving my partner even when I hate him.

It's not just me. I get letters every week from people who want to know how to run their relationships better. I talk to friends, colleagues – and strangers on trains – who are happy enough, but want more than that.

It's not our fault. We ask a lot of love nowadays – more even than we did when John and Claire got married. We expect to be partners and lovers, sweethearts and best friends – for life. And we expect to do it all by instinct. If we don't, we feel failures because love nowadays is seen as easy, easy, easy.

It's time to admit that actually love is *not* easy, that it doesn't come naturally. And that though we're desperate to have it succeed, no one ever explains just how to do that.

No one ever tells us the realistic, sometimes hard, truth about relationships.

No one ever shows us how to make love work.

If you want to know how to make love work, read this book.

It tells you what you need to know and what you need to do in the most common situations you'll meet in your relationship. It gives you a practical working plan to sort out the issues as you face them. It gives you stories, lessons and insights gathered from love, from life – and most of all from couples who've learned the hard way how to make their relationhips work.

A lot of what's in here may seem tough and unidealistic. It is. It's real statements about real love in today's tough world – no romantic visions, no pulled punches. If you take these ideas on board and use them, then if it is at all possible for you to make love work, you will.

Because I really believe that, despite everything, ordinary people can, like John and Claire, create extraordinary relationships.

We all want such relationships. We deserve them. And the reason we find it hard to have them is not because there's anything wrong or bad about us. It's because we've never been shown how to do it.

Once we've been shown how to love, we'll be able to love.

Simple truth about love

If the two of you are finding love challenging at the
moment.

If it's all not quite as exciting as it was. If it's all not
quite as easy as it was.

That's great.

It means you're starting to tackle the real issues.

You're starting to experience real love.

Read this when the excitement is fading

The first time I went to the pantomime was the best – and then the worst – day of my childhood.

I was seven years old, and an aunt of mine had organized a trip for all her nephews and nieces – a staggering eleven of us. We filled two cars. We wore our best clothes. We laughed till we got overexcited. We ate chocolates till we felt sick. And all that was before the performance.

When the curtain went up, I burst into tears. Not tears of grief, but tears of nervous joy. It was my first theatre visit, and I'd never seen anything like it in my life. The lights, the constantly changing scenery, the sparkling costumes, the songs, the dances, the better-than-perfect world. For two hours I sat holding my breath, aware of nothing but what was happening on stage.

And then the curtain came down, and we clapped and clapped, and then we put our coats on and began to leave, enchanted.

As we pushed our way through the exit doors and onto the wintery, rain-swept streets of Liverpool, I burst into tears again. And this time, it was serious.

I wanted the performance to go on and on. I didn't want to leave the theatre, ever. I certainly didn't want to be back in real life. I cried all the way back home in the car, all the way through the celebration tea, and all the way home to bed ...

There's a point in every relationship where you come out of the theatre and into the rain.

It's the first big crisis, and it can make or break you. And it's the first big realization you need if you're going to be able to love.

A few months in ... or after the honeymoon ... or during a major row ... or maybe just the first time you see your partner as a man who can make mistakes, what was sparkling and shiny and exciting and wonderful turns into something much more everyday, down-to-earth and normal. What was completely perfect and effortless and full of miraculous possibilities shifts into something that has its challenges, its limitations and its problems.

Because unless you're one of these very rare couples who got together through practicality or friendship rather than through emotion or lust, you fell for your partner in a huge and important leap. But over time, in another equally important leap, you fall again – out of that feeling, that first infatuation.

You take off the rose-coloured glasses and start to see your relationship for real.

What no one tells you at this point is that it's completely normal. Don't panic. First infatuation fades. Because like any performance, it isn't actually real.

Biologically, it's an altered state, a hormonal surge that brings two people together, and keeps them together until they've made love and made babies. And so whether or not you actually do make babies, that first phase eventually fades – not always completely, but always noticeably.

Though it can feel a little bit as if you are dying.

Because when you first fell for your partner, you saw him as a god – when in fact he's just a very human man. When you first had sex with your partner, you thought that it was going to be ecstasy day after day – when in fact sometimes it's quite nice and sometimes it's a strain. And yes, in the early months you thought your relationship was the answer to every problem you'd ever had – when in fact it's a whole new set of extremely difficult questions.

That's the first realization. The second is this:

It is possible to break through to a new sort of relationship, to build a stronger, deeper, and in the end, better love from the foundations of the old excitement. It is possible to turn the euphoric highs into a constant deep contentment. To turn the sense of possibility into a certainty that lasts you through life. And to use your relationship not just to make each other happy but also more effective and fulfilled – the best partners and the best people you can be.

But you do need to be brave. Whether you're going through this transition now, or have it ahead of you, or are looking back at it, you need courage.

Because in the end you'll have to look across at your partner and see another ordinary human being. You'll have to look round at your relationship and see real life.

And then you'll have to start learning how to love.

Here are four things to tell yourself when the excitement's fading:

♥ First passion is a drug, biologically and emotionally. We may enjoy being addicted, but long-term its effect will fade.

♥ Everyone, at some time, feels like this. It doesn't mean we're failing or that we have to split up.

♥ We can do it. The fact that we've lasted this long means we can move on and make something even more worthwhile.

♥ This is the end of first attraction. But it could be the start of life-long loving.

Simple truth about love

When you first love, your needs are strong but surface. Excitement. Attention. Romance. Sex.

When love gets real and long-term, you start meeting deeper needs. Security. Appreciation. Acceptance. Cooperation. Fulfilment.

These needs are vital. They're transforming. And they're incredibly difficult to do.

That's why when love goes right, it can make you utterly happy.

When love goes wrong it can break you — utterly.

Read this if you're not secure in your love

My next-door neighbour was always a timid man. But he grew positively paranoid after he retired.

He had four separate locks and chains on the front door, and three on the back. Every single window had one of those safety handles that you need a special key to open. The burglar alarm was set each night, so that if you wanted a glass of water, all hell was let loose as you tiptoed down to the kitchen.

Even so, my next-door neighbour still worried. He was so terrified of being burgled that he hated going out, and he held back from doing almost everything in life that might have given him a little bit of pleasure. In the end, of course, he lived safely and securely in his fortified house until he died of old age. But almost his last words to me were, 'Something might happen.'

I'm not mocking him. He's absolutely right. Something might well happen.There are burglars, and muggers, and things that go bump in the night, every night. And nothing's more frightening than the fear that you're going to lose your love.

And here's the hard bit: It could well happen.

Particularly once the first excitement fades and the challenges start to kick in, there'll be times when the foundations of your relationship get shaken. When life bugs you and you aren't the centre of each other's attention any more. When you start to bug each other and your commitment starts to slide.

Lots of us, when we first realize this, start going into over-drive to protect our love. Like my next-door neighbour, we bolt the doors. And like him, we completely undermine our chances of getting a life.

We worry and fret about whether that first excitement will last – and when it doesn't, we think everything's lost. We hedge our relationship round with demands and boundaries – and then get bewildered when our partner tries to escape. We listen to our partner's genuine promises, put them to the test a thousand times – and then wonder why our relationship self-destructs. Or we do absolutely everything and anything to keep our relationship going – and then get surprised when our partner takes us for granted.

If you spend your time worrying that your love will be destroyed, then ironically, you're half way to destroying it. Even if you don't destroy it, you've got a good chance of strangling its potential at birth.

Because if you want to have a good relationship, let alone have a life, you need to have your sense of security on the inside rather than trying to bolt it on from the outside.

It will help to hang on to these three realizations:

♥ Love will change, and good times will turn to bad times. But almost always, they'll turn to good times again. And if you build your relationship to be strong, you can ride that out.

♥ Your partner will change, will sometimes feel so strongly about you that it hurts, and other times will keep what he feels for you warm but unnoticeable, in the background. And just sometimes, he'll hate you. But if you can let love ebb just slightly and still not panic, then it will flow again.

♥ If your partner did leave, you would almost certainly pull through. Yes, it would hurt. But most people who suffer a breakup start to recover within six months. Almost always, you will too. You have more strength than you realize.

It may feel as if you're putting your relationship at risk to believe that you could survive without it.
But you're putting it much more at risk by believing that without it, you'd die.

Read this when you need a confidence boost

If you need to feel more certain that you can make your love work, then realize this.

There are two of you in your relationship. But just one of you can change everything.

Actually, you already know this. There've been times when just one of you has said something or done something that's completely knocked both of you sideways or taken you to the very edge.

Or, there've been times when just one of you has turned everything round. A word, a glance, a kiss, a hug – or a steady stream of support or love. One of you has been taking the strain or has taken the initiative. And it's made all the difference.

Just at the moment, the power to make the difference in your relationship lies with you. Not because you're the only important one in your partnership. But because you're the one who's inputting energy, commitment, enthusiasm – and particularly as a woman, inputting a deep knowledge and mastery of emotions and relationships.

Yes, your partner may be well up for whatever you're going to suggest – and over time, he'll start to add his energy to your effort.

But the bottom line is that here and now, you're the one who's reading this book.

So you can make the first move. You don't have to wait for your partner to shift, or even to want to shift. You can make things happen as soon as you want.

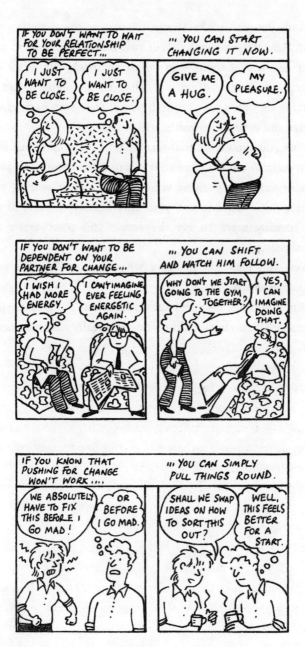

And, you can make things happen in the direction you want. Research suggests that if two people are close to each other and one of them alters their approach, the other will naturally follow, instinctively alter their approach too. So amazing though it may seem, if you change your partner will change and your relationship will change ...

Plus you can create that change positively and with little or no pain. You don't have to try to make love work by sheer force of emotion, pushing your partner and pressuring your relationship. You can use your intelligence, your skill and your commitment to get the result you want easily and effortlessly.

Yes, you may feel insecure when you realize that what happens is down to you.

But don't you also feel reassured when you realize that, because it's down to you, things can now really start happening?

Read this when you want to create a solid foundation

There can't be many people in the world who haven't heard of Paul McCartney and his wife Linda. And of Linda's tragic death of cancer in 1998.

Apparently when they met, they made an unofficial vow to each other, and kept it over their years together. It was this:

'I will never put you down'

That promise didn't just mean that Paul and Linda would never pull the rug out from under each other by criticizing, blaming, having a go.

It also meant that they would always keep each other safe, defend each other, nurture each other, and carry each other safely through life.

It's an essential.

Of course, you can't protect each other from everything the world has to throw at you. The McCartneys didn't protect each other from media criticism, or from the ups and downs of their day-to-day life. And, though Paul lay beside Linda on her death bed and cuddled her to stop her being frightened, in the end he couldn't stop her dying of cancer.

But what Paul and Linda could do was give each other basic safety and security.

To keep interacting even when it was tempting to cut off. To stay involved emotionally even when it started to hurt. To keep communicating even when tempted to try and bring each other to heel by sulking. To hang in there even when tempted to try and control each other by threatening to leave.

Because they knew that sort of security gave them the space to really love each other. To conduct their relationship cleanly and honestly without being frightened that the other one would run away or turn away. To keep developing as individuals because they had a stable basis of partnership security.

If you want to give your partner and your relationship a solid foundation, start by digging deep to offer as much security as you can. As far as possible ...

♥ ... never pull back verbally, or stop talking. Keep the connection.

♥ ... never pull back physically. If you don't want sex, offer cuddles and affection.

♥ ... never pull back emotionally. The minute you feel separate, get close again.

♥ ... never use the threat of leaving as a weapon. If you're going to leave, leave. If you're not, don't threaten it for effect.

♥ ... above all, never put your partner down.

Simple truth about love

Fact – short-term, you'll feel most secure with some-one similar to you. Like attracts like.

Fact – long-term, you'll make a better, happier relationship with someone whose differences complement yours. Opposites attract.

To make love work, all you have to do ...

... is sort that contradiction!

Read this if you wish he was more like you

Just occasionally, when I'm channel-hopping, I catch a few minutes of a sci-fi horror movie. Some deadly alien nation infiltrates our human bodies and turns us into clones. Everyone the same. Replicas. Marching with identical steps off into a terrifying future. Ugh!

So why is it that when it comes to love, what we really want is a clone?

What we really want is someone who's the same as we are – thinking, speaking, doing. Who'll see the world our way, and do things our way.

Because we feel that's the way things should be. Our way.

But everyone's different. Every human being has a unique upbringing – is a unique person. That means that when we search for our doppelganger, we don't find them.

What we do find is someone who excites us physically and mentally. And at first their differences don't matter. Even if they do, this person approves of us, likes us. So we feel safe, happy, OK. Clones at last.

And then, over time, the differences start to bite. We do things one way and our partner another. We don't see eye to eye. We make different decisions. We have different tastes. We even react differently to the basic joys and sorrows of life.

When we stand together and look over a romantic river setting, one of us notices the moonlight dappling on the water ... and the other of us notices the exact technical specification of the sails on the third boat from the left.

Your partner doesn't understand you. And it hurts.

It hurts because the message you get is that your way is wrong, and so you're wrong. Or alternatively, that your partner's wrong and you're wrong for staying with him. So you have to give in to his approach, or persuade him to yours.

But there's another way of looking at it all. You can see the whole thing not as a problem but as an opportunity. And if you do, then the variations in your relationship will stop being so threatening – and you'll stop feeling so threatened. (And so will your partner.)

Your differences may not mean one of you is wrong – but that both of you are right.

You may think that given two ways of thinking, of doing, of feeling, one of them's going to be less effective. But this isn't a case of 'either ... or'. Almost always, when you and your partner are different, both ways are useful. If they hadn't been, you wouldn't each have used them so much down the years.

So he's an optimist and you're a pessimist, or vice versa. That's fine. It means that one of you gets enthusiastic about things, while the other of you mine-detects for problems. But there's no need to feel bad or invalid. Your way is right. So is your partner's. Together, you're doubly right.

Your differences may not be a limitation – but an expansion of possibilities.

It can feel as if each of you is demanding that the other change, be different, do things another way. But you don't have to to do things your partner's way – just as he doesn't have to do things your way. You can both stick to your own ways.

And then – and here's the good bit – you can borrow each other's ways, add on each other's strategies to broaden your repertoire. So he's a party animal – you can learn from him to be sociable when you want to be. So you enjoy your own company – he can learn from you to be self-sufficient when he needs to be.

Your differences may not mean you have to compete, but that you can compensate.

If you use your differences cooperatively, you can make life easier for both of you by filling in each other's gaps. If one of you has a weakness, the other may well have a strength.

So one of you always forgets to send birthday cards – but that's not a problem because the other always remembers. And when it comes to map reading, one of you has a blind spot – but the other can do it blindfold. Your differences will make you more effective in the world together than apart. An accelerator works better if it has a brake.

(And there's no need to follow gender stereotypes here – in one of the happiest couples I know, the man is good at house-keeping, the woman at book-keeping. So he does the dishes. And she does the accounts.)

Because there's a very good reason why you and your part-ner aren't the same, aren't clones, and it's this. Sameness makes for weakness. But variation – in partnerships as well as in gene pools – makes for strength, power and capability.

So the next time you wish your partner was more like you, don't get mad.

Get grateful. He's not a clone.

Read this if you feel so different it hurts

The Channel Tunnel. The Skye Bridge. Recently the whole world seems to be joining up. One place to another. One country to another.

Even two decades ago, no one thought these links were possible. Then realization dawned, and was slowly turned into action as concrete and steel got slung across valleys, thrust through mountains, and tunnelled through sheer rock. Slowly but surely, we're joining up the dots.

If you and your partner are finding your differences a real problem ... if you irritate and nag and blame each other ... if you argue over your different world views ... if you feel so different it hurts ... then you need to actively start joining up the dots.

Understanding each other's experiences. Sympathizing with each other's problems. Linking your individual styles and approaches in a practical way. Bringing your varying views together. Constructing tunnels. Building bridges.

Here's an example that involves two friends of mine. Trivial, but it makes the point. They have a thatched cottage – safe but not somewhere you'd want to have a fire. When they first moved in, they'd have running battles about the smoke detectors – of which there are four. He'd position them. She, in the course of shifting furniture or tidying up, would reposition them. When she did, he'd reposition them again. And so on.

As they tell it, it took years of this kind of minor aggravation before one of them thought to say 'Why do you do that?' and for her to discover that there was rhyme and reason to his actions – smoke alarms only work in certain positions. While he in turn discovered that she knew next to nothing about the dynamics of smoke and so didn't appreciate his rhyme and reason.

Once he understood that her repositioning was from ignorance, he relaxed.

Once she understood that his repositioning was from knowledge, so did she ...

If either of you gets irritated with the other – over small things like smoke alarms, or big things like how to bring up the kids – it's probably because you're different and you haven't understood each other yet. If you can ask questions to start understanding, it will immediately get easier.

It will help to explain your differences. Because when something's named and explained, it loses its threat. So don't defend your approach, or attack your partner, or go into overdrive to apologize for what you're doing. Instead, calmly and clearly explain why you do what you do – and watch him take things on board much more easily.

It'll also help to explore differences. If you start feeling bad about something your partner's doing that's different from the way you'd do it, find out what his thinking is. These five questions will help you explore:

♥ What – What's the reason behind your doing that?
♥ Where – Where did you learn to do it that way?
♥ When – When did you realize that was the way to do it?
♥ Who – Who showed you that?
♥ How – How do you know to do it like that?

Plus, it will help to appreciate each other's differences. Lots of bad feeling happens because people get defensive – they feel that if they're doing something different, they must be getting it wrong. If they feel appreciated in what they're doing, the bad feeling dissolves, along with the potential for a row. So tell your partner what you like about the fact he's different – and encourage him to return the favour.

Remember. What you do always affects your partner. So the bottom line is this. The more you understand his ways of doing things, the more he'll understand yours.

The more you understand each other, the more you'll want to understand.

Simple truth about love

There's only one thing worse than feeling negative about how different your partner is from you.

And that's realizing that he feels just as negative about how different you are from him.

There's only one thing better than appreciating the fact that your partner is different from you.

And that's telling each other how much you appreciate your individual differences.

Read this when you're tempted to have a go at him

Jannie and her boyfriend had been going out for three and a half months when they decided to take a break away; their first together, driving round Italy and seeing all their favourite places. A dream holiday.

Except for the daily nightmare. Each evening, after a hot and hard day's sightseeing, they'd head for whatever town they'd booked in to stay the night. They'd hit the autostrada. Usually hit five lanes of traffic. Miss the turnoff. Try to find the hotel. Get lost. Get fratched. End up rowing. And then take until the following morning to get back to feeling good again.

As they tell it now, they dined in sullen silence in half the hill towns of Central Italy.

Then one day, stuck in the Florence rush hour, and clutching the driving wheel for grim death, Jannie glanced sideways at Ned as he stared down at the map and desperately tried to work out where they were. He looked tired. Jannie says he looked, somehow, defeated.

Now normally, at this point, she would have had a go at him. But this time, instead of the critical thoughts that were tumbling through her head, she found herself thinking 'He's got us here ... even in this traffic.' And instead of the bitter riposte that was hovering on her lips, she found herself saying 'It's fine, love. You're doing fine ... you're doing really well ...'

Jannie says that at that moment, she saw Ned's whole body respond. He suddenly lost his defeated look, his face relaxed, his body followed. He took a deep breath, looked over at her smiled and said 'Thanks', and went back to the map.

Jannie didn't know quite what she'd done at that point. But she knew that she'd done something very important. Something that would make a difference to their relationship in more contexts than just the Florence rush hour. And strangely enough, there was no row that night ...

Inside that partner of yours is, actually, someone who feels he's messing up a lot of the time.

Yes, he may seem self-confident. Or defensive. Or sometimes just plain stroppy. But actually, he looks in the mirror each morning and sees mistakes. Looks back over the day and sees failings. Often doesn't notice he's getting it right because he's too busy noticing when he gets it wrong. And who when he does get it wrong, like you, needs more anything to be told what he's getting right.

Knowing you're OK is one of the most basic needs human beings have. So it will help if you can find the strength to positively appreciate your partner – because he succeeded, because he triumphed – or better still, just because he tried.

Don't do it falsely – he'll know if you're just complimenting him for effect.

Don't do it forcibly – he won't hear it if you try relentless celebration.

And don't just do it from time to time. Of course use appreciation to avert an occasional crisis, as Jannie did. But also dripfeed appreciation on a daily basis. Perhaps add to something he already feels good about. Certainly turn round any self-putdowns that he comes up with. And always let your body language as well as your words bring home the message.

love coach

It may come as a shock to your partner – at first he may even bridle at your positivity. But that's because he isn't used to it, not because he doesn't need it.

Just carry on, regularly and lovingly, telling him what's right rather than what's wrong. It may take weeks, or months, but it will make a difference. He'll feel better about himself, better about the relationship, better about you.

Finally, remember this. A human brain may need as many as five positive messages to counteract the effect of a single negative one.

Your partner probably received several thousand negative messages before he even started school. Not to mention the ones he got while he was growing up ... the ones he gets when he's at work ... and – let's face it – the ones he's got from love relationships.

So start appreciating him now. He's got a lot of catching up to do ...

Read this when you're tempted to insult him

Some words have the power to kill. They go right to the heart of a partner's weakest spots, and turn the knife.

Because there are some things you can say that will reflect your partner's deepest self-doubts with horrible accuracy. To someone else they may be utterly harmless. But to your partner they'll pinpoint the exact ways in which he feels he's lacking. So your partner will hear his worst fears put into words by someone he thought loved him.

If your partner believes deep down that he's not as intelligent as you are, the killer words might be, 'You're so stupid' . If he suspects he's not expert sexually, the words might be 'You're rubbish in bed'.

'You're fat ... you're boring ... you're useless ... you're a terrible parent ... you're going bald'. You almost certainly know the killer words and phrases in your relationship, because you almost certainly know your partner better than anyone else does.

So like it or not, you have the power to destroy, by saying these things when you're angry, when you're upset. Or most hurtful of all, when you're just not thinking.

Once these words are out, it's almost impossible to undo the damage they cause. Because your partner will never be able to forget that some part of you thought the worst of them.

So not only will he never be able to feel the same again about you.

But worse still, he'll never be able to feel the same again about himself.

Read this when you want to give him an ego boost

Here's a neat trick for when you really want to give your partner the message that you rate him.

Smile.

Sneaky, huh? Manipulative. Underhand. It seems so obvious that you can't believe it could have an effect.

But a smile not only makes you feel good. It also tells your partner two things.

First and most directly it will tell him you approve of him – and that will make him feel good.

But second, your smile will tell your partner that you're happy. And that, in a roundabout way, will make him feel doubly good. Because most men (and women) get their deepest sense of achievement from knowing that the person they love is happy. They can metaphorically relax then; they've done their job.

Of course, this won't work if you give a grudging smile, a half-hearted smile. Nor a smile just to please or keep him sweet – we're absolutely not talking 'give us a smile then, darlin'.'

But if you give a full-on energetic smile – or even any genuine smile, however weary – it will make a difference. Do it, and even a partner who's feeling low will start to feel good about himself and about you.

Too many couples make the mistake of thinking that because they love each other, they don't need to show that they like each other.

Read this if you want to help him fulfil his potential

Until I was nine years old, I didn't know there was anything wrong about succeeding.

I grew up in a family where you did your best. And if you didn't come first, or top, that was fine. But if you did, that was fine too. Winning prizes was a reason for celebration. Being good at something meant you got cuddles and praise.

Then one day at school – I remember we were all painting pictures in the art room – the headmistress came in. She stopped the class, and announced that I'd won a writing competition. The prize, a trip abroad. What an honour for the school. How proud they all were of me.

That lunchhour, I got bullied in the playground.

I didn't learn my lesson right away, of course. I won another competition, got bullied again. Came top in English and got bullied for that. And slowly learned to keep my head down and my profile low. Learned to do my best, but let that best be an average best. Tall poppies get cut down fast and early.

And so by the time I met my husband, Ian, I was in an average job in an average situation – and I don't think I'd had an achievement-orientated thought in ten years. I just didn't see myself as someone who did well. So I didn't.

There wasn't any one thing Ian did to change that, no overnight miracle. It was just a drip feed of appreciation that started to change my mind. Like him consistently telling me that I could write. Like him supporting me when I thought about starting a book. Like him encouraging me to approach publishers and find an agent. And like him making me feel that even if everyone in the world tried to cut me down again, he'd stand alongside me and fight.

Ian helped me unlearn what I'd taken on board so completely as a child – that doing well was dangerous. He helped me relearn what I was capable of doing. And being.

If you choose, you can do for your partner what Ian did for me. Beyond your relationship, beyond the daily give and take, you can do something more.

If you want, you can help him unlearn all sorts of non-useful things that he took on board as a child. Things that make him feel bad about himself. Things that hold him back. Things that make him unhappy.

And after you've helped your partner unlearn, then you can help him relearn. That he's clever, when he always thought he was thick. That he's capable, when he always thought he couldn't get his act together. That he's important, when he always thought that actually, he was pretty low down in the heap.

There's no need to make big statements. Relearning is a subtle process. But a dripfeed of positivity and belief can, over time, help him relearn these messages:

That he's good at things

People often learn to hide what they're good at, to play it down, to subvert it. If they don't, they get told off for boasting or put down through envy. So your partner may have got to a point where he's actually forgotten he has any talents, and thinks of himself as average or even as a failure.

If you get uneasy or undermine his successes, you'll just hammer the lesson home. If you tell him what he's good at, he'll get the confidence to reclaim his strengths, and shine.

That he's right

Parents, teachers, big brothers, employers ... everyone higher in the pecking order will tell a person they're wrong. So your partner may grow up believing that whatever he thinks is bound to be somehow flawed – and lose trust in his own thoughts and feelings.

If you get into the habit of querying his viewpoint or rubbishing his ideas, he'll continue to learn the lesson – with resulting wobbles or defensiveness. If you notice where he gets it right, he'll start to feel more at ease with himself and more able to deal with the world in a confident way.

That he's worth it

As a child, your partner may have learned that he doesn't actually deserve to have anything. And that may mean that he rushes in aggressively to grab, or tries to manipulate you,

in order to get things.

If you add to his impression that nothing will come his way by right, however well he does, then he'll carry on behaving badly. But if you give him the message that you believe he deserves the best, then he'll start to believe it too – and will gradually get much more at ease with himself.

That he can stand up for his rights

Boys in particular are expected to handle conflict well – fights in the playground, bullying at school. So your partner may have learned to be aggressive at any hint of trouble – or to back down immediately. Then as an adult, he may overreact to confrontation or be uneasy around it.

If you can stand beside him when he stands up for his rights, he'll start to realize he has the resources to face challenging situations easily and to cope with them elegantly.

Read this if you want to make your relationship a place to grow

You will both change and develop by being with each other. But be careful.

Because you may not always develop positively. Over time, your relationship may actually change you for the worse.

♥ If your relationship becomes a place of unappreciation then you'll lose confidence and feel depressed.

♥ If it becomes a place of insecurity then one or both of you will become vulnerable

♥ If it becomes a place of power-struggle you'll end up defeated, or you'll rebel.

♥ If it becomes a place of unmet needs you'll become resentful and demanding.

♥ If it becomes a place of rejection you'll either strike back or lose heart.

♥ It doesn't have to be like that.

None of these disasters need happen if you make your relationship a place where you can both develop positively.

♥ If you create a climate of appreciating each other – so you become self-confident and enthusiastic.

♥ Create a climate of offering each other security – so you become strong and stable.

♥ Create a climate of cooperating together, so you become a working team.

♥ Create a climate of meeting each other's needs – so you become satisfied and fulfilled.
♥ Create a climate of accepting – so you're able to feel good about who you really are.

love coach

Simple truth about love

If you know your partner loves you, don't you feel good about yourself? Don't you feel wonderful, marvellous and superb?

Well, there's the good news and the bad news.

The good news is that you're already wonderful, marvellous and superb. Even if your partner doesn't love you.

The bad news is that it often doesn't seem like that at the time.

Read this if you're tempted to give yourself a hard time

If you want to reach the Golden Gallery in the Dome of St Paul's cathedral, you need to climb exactly 538 steps. And one hot day a few summers ago, at around step 210, I decided that my constant mental refrain 'I'm not up to this' was absolutely correct.

My lungs, calves and thighs gave me a spontaneous round of applause as I stopped for breath, finally admitted failure, and turned to go back down again.

Just then, someone come slowly up the stairs below me. He was 80 if he was a day, white-haired, slightly stooped, and gasping as much as I was. But as he passed me – with a smile – I could just hear the words 'doing fine ... doing OK ... keeping going ... getting there ...'.

I got the message.

As I turned round again and carried on up, I still stopped for breath every few steps. But now I kept telling myself what I was getting right rather than what I was getting wrong.

At the top, the old man and I stood beside each other at the railing and admired the view over London together.

What I learned from that man was this. Appreciating yourself works. Of course it goes against the human grain to tell yourself how well you're doing – particularly if you don't seem to be doing well at all. But actually, concentrating on what I was getting right didn't make me bigheaded – it gave me energy, made me feel good, kept me going. While telling myself how badly I was doing just made me feel like giving up.

If you want good feeling in your relationship in general, then you need to give lots of good feeling to yourself in particular, not just to your partner or your children.

You deserve it – women so often put themselves at the bottom of the list when appreciation is being handed out.

But also, your relationship deserves it. The best lovers feel good about themselves and what they do. If within the context of your relationship, and over the course of your relationship, you feel better and better about yourself, then you'll be a more fulfilling partner. As well as a more fulfilled person.

Here are ten ways to make love work by loving yourself:

♥ Notice when you're doing well and feel good about it.

♥ If you feel you're not doing well, feel good about the fact that you're trying.

♥ When you don't get a result, remember that you did your best.

♥ When someone says something good about you, say 'thank you' – without hesitating, flinching or laughing it off.

♥ When your partner says something good about you, show him how happy it makes you – so he learns to do it more.

♥ When your partner says something bad about you, see that as his problem, not yours.

♥ Really take on board the fact that you need five self-congratulations to erase the draining effect of one self-put down.

♥ If you do mess up, put it in context. You probably did at least a thousand things right before you did that one thing wrong.

♥ If you really, really mess up, think how much better you'll do next time. Well, you certainly won't make that same mistake again, will you?

♥ Remember that the amount you can feel good about someone else is in direct proportion to the amount you feel good about yourself.

Read this if you feel he never appreciates you

Of course you need your partner to tell you he loves you.

But you also need him to tell you why he loves you.

Even if you're incredibly self-confident inside, you deserve to be loved by someone who's certain about your strengths, your talents, your uniqueness. Who gets turned on sexually or emotionally by your hair ... or your sense of humour ... or your confidence ... or even your driving style!

If your partner can't, or doesn't, tell you how he loves you, it can feel like living in an emotional desert. You can get almost physically thirsty for appreciation

If you feel thirsty in your relationship, ask yourself two questions:

First, does your partner actually appreciate you? If the answer is no, then you've got a problem. If for some reason he's forgotten what he liked about you and what he loved about you, then you probably don't have much of a relationship left. And you'll have to decide for yourself what that means for your relationship.

Or is it that your partner simply doesn't know how to tell you he appreciates you? Because often what seems to be a partner not appreciating is actually a partner not communicating. He doesn't have the words. Or he doesn't realize you need to hear them. Or he doesn't realize you need to hear them regularly in order to really believe them.

And that if you don't hear them regularly, it's a bit like watering a plant once a year. Quite simply, you won't survive.

You are not a cactus.

If your partner appreciates you, but isn't able to show it, here are four ways to coach him along:

♥ Appreciate him. He will respond. He will like it. And he will – in time – learn to return the favour.

♥ When you need to be appreciated, ask him to do it. Directly, clearly, positively ask.

♥ Give him ways to show he appreciates you. Tell him what words to use. Show him what body language to use.

♥ Whenever he does appreciate you, reward him. Tell him and show him clearly how very good it makes you feel.

Simple truth about love

Love isn't just appreciating each other when you get it right.

It's sticking with it when you get it wrong.

Love isn't just enjoying each other when things are easy.

It's accepting each other even when the going gets tough.

Read this when he gets on your nerves

One of the wisest women I know had a lovely phrase that she used now and again. It came into its own if she met any couple where there was obvious tension or friction.

She'd watch them sympathetically as they tried to put on a brave face in public. And when they'd left, she'd say 'mmm ... those two have worn their love away ...'.

Because over time, however committed you are, you can quite simply wear away the affection and the tolerance. It's not that there's been any kind of problem or crisis. It's just that your different ways of doing things have rubbed up against each other. Or you've lived too long with the same habits and personalities. You've stopped really appreciating each other, started finding each other abrasive, begun to get on each other's nerves.

It'll show. Even if you try to hide it, it'll show. In the way you feel about each other – not quite so relaxed, not quite so trusting. In the way you treat each other – still caring, but with sideways glances, tension around the mouth, a tendency to snap. And all these things will, of course, wear away your love even more.

It's a big leap, an act of real bravery, to let surface annoyance drop away and real tolerance come back. To stop being annoyed, and instead be sympathetic. In short, to accept who your partner really is on a minute to minute level. But it is possible, even after years of irritation, to simply do it. And if you can do it, and even if in the beginning only one of you can do it, then it will make a difference.

The friction and abrasiveness between you will start to fade. And underneath the emotional scars, the healthy relationship will start to grow back. You'll begin to remember what it was you liked about each other.

So even if at first you have to make an effort, positively accept your partner.

Accept him by the way you look at him, directly and as if you like what you see. New, infatuated lovers spend literally hours gazing into each other's eyes – so if you want to give your partner the signal that you still care, spend time doing just that. Maybe in bed in the morning. Maybe when you're cuddling up on the sofa. Or maybe just when you pass in the hall.

Accept him by the way you talk to him, warmly, and as if you appreciate what you hear. So use words that signal you accept him, 'It's fine, that's great, no problem'. And put some meaning into it. If your partner hears enthusiasm in your voice, he'll respond to that.

And accept him by the way you touch him, affectionately and as if you love what you feel. Touch is our first-experienced sense, the one that comforts us even in major crises. So touch your partner lots, to celebrate, to commiserate – or for no reason at all.

As always, of course, there's a bonus.

If you accept your partner, he'll find it easier to accept and love himself.

If he accepts himself, he'll find it easier to accept and love you.

Read this when he makes a mistake

The first time my husband Ian and I ever went out together, we actually stayed in. He said he'd cook a meal, I went round to his flat, we ended up making vegetable stir fry in his tiny bedsit kitchen. Two of us, side by side at the draining board, chopping vegetables like there was no tomorrow.

We were so high on lust and the possibilities of a new relationship, that we couldn't pass without touching each other. We were so distracted it was a wonder one of us didn't slice a finger off.

As each portion of vegetables got chopped, we put them aside to wait for the actual frying. And we put them into a wonderful green ceramic bowl that Ian said was the most precious thing he owned. He'd been given it by an exflatmate, a potter; he showed me the pattern on the glaze, and the marks where her fingers had dug in. I thought it was beautiful – and that he was beautiful for loving it.

We'd done the carrots, and the mushrooms, and I was just turning to slide them from the chopping board into the green bowl. Now, I'm not the most coordinated bunny in the world, and that day I excelled myself. I tipped everything sideways, and of course, it happened.

The bowl fell onto the floor.

Ian says now that he can still remember me standing there frozen like a rabbit in car headlights, looking at the thousand green pieces and waiting for his reaction. What I remember is thinking that he must be either furious or gutted. I lifted my head and waited for at best a forced smile, at worst a howl.

He said slowly 'Well ... you didn't mean it, did you?.'

I was astounded. Because even though he must have felt terrible about what had happened, that didn't mean he felt terrible about me. He accepted that I'd done my best. He accepted that I made mistakes. He accepted me.

It was at this point that I thought I might like to stay with the guy for a while.

Because absolutely the best thing anyone can do for us is to accept us even when we get it wrong. To see us mess up. To see us foul up. To see us clearly without the rose-coloured glasses or even the lust. And still not reject us.

Knowing that someone who loves us also accepts us – and our mistakes – is an amazing experience. We immediately feel secure on a level we've never felt before. We start to realize that we don't have to try, that we can relax and just be ourselves. The stress fades away, we get more energy, we have more focus. We not only feel better, we get better at what we do.

So of course be tolerant and supportive of your partner over big things, where you feel he needs your love because he's going through a crisis. But also have the courage to tolerate and support him in the small things, the day-to-day things, the things that bug you, the broken bowls of life.

That way, every time he's with you, he'll feel accepted for who he is. He'll start to feel secure, and worthwhile. He'll start to see himself as a valid person. He'll start to believe he's OK.

It will be you who's made that happen.

Read this if you can't accept his mistakes

When things are going well, it's easy to accept your partner – tolerate him, support him, even appreciate him.

But when what he does, or what he is, has upset or hurt you, it's tempting to hurt back. Every cell in your body wants to lash out, to nag, to blame, to shout, to reject. So why shouldn't you?

Here are some of the objections people come up with when it's hard to accept:

If my partner is behaving badly surely he needs telling, not accepting?

If what you mean by 'behaving badly' is drugs, abuse or violence, then telling won't work. You need to take serious action: get support for you, get support for him, lay down some bottom-line requirements from you to him, or leave.

If what you mean by 'behaving badly' is that your partner has simply messed up without meaning to, then in fact, telling still won't work. There's a mysterious process in human nature that makes people repeat unintentional mistakes if they're blamed for them. (Conversly, if those unintentional mistakes are commiserated, and support is given to get things right, then people mysteriously tend to get things right next time.)

If what you mean by 'behaving badly' is that your partner's done something to wind you up, or refused you something you want, then once again 'telling' won't work. Explaining might work ... or talking about what you need ... or negotiating so that you both get what you want. But 'telling' – that blend of nagging and blaming and demanding that's the very opposite of accepting – is counterproductive whoever's doing it. Because it always makes both of you feel bad. And it almost always makes both of you dig your heels in.

Hold on a minute though – what's in it for me?

When you accept your partner, you do two things that will give you a definite – though not immediate – benefit.

First, you start to set up a climate of acceptance that makes it more likely that your partner will accept you on a day to day basis – tolerate your shortcomings, put up with the ways in which you irritate him. Which, admit it, you sometimes do.

Second, accepting a partner's shortcomings creates a slow but definite change in him. When someone is accepted, he (or she) becomes more able to give love as well as get it. Because when people don't have to work so hard on accepting themselves from the inside, they have more acceptance left to give away on the outside.

This isn't theory. This works. Unless people are incapable of ever forming a good intimate relationship, then the more they're accepted, the more they can show their love.

So unless your partner is actually incapable of forming a good intimate relationship – and if he is incapable, then leave, because you deserve better – then the more you accept him, the more he'll be able to love you.

But my partner doesn't accept me. So why on earth should I accept him?

If your partner doesn't accept you, that's probably because he doesn't realize that accepting works. He still thinks that to get what he wants in the relationship, he needs to tell you the minute you do anything that doesn't sit easily with him. So he may blame you if you irritate him, throw a tantrum if you get it wrong, back off if you mess up.

In fact, he's misunderstood the way the world really operates. Well, hasn't he? Check it out. When are you more likely to behave well towards your partner, more likely to work to sort things out, more likely to want to do right by him?

When he nags and blames you? Or when he supports, encourages and hangs on in there?

Have I made my point?

So explain all this to your partner. Or show him. Show him that accepting gets a better result than not accepting, that behaving calmly and supportively gets both of you motivated to make things work.

It will feel hard, and it may be hard – but you can do it.

And if you do it, it will get results.

Simple truth about love

If you feel bad about your partner, then by all means try to accept him. But be aware that that's only the first step.

Because when you really accept your partner, then you don't feel bad about him. Or his thoughts. Or his actions. Or his feelings.

If you accept him, you realize they're all part of a very human package.

They're not perfect. But they're him.

Read this when he gets emotional

My friend Steve is a big guy. Six foot three and hefty with it – he used to play lock forward for his local amateur team. And one of the things that attracted his wife Kate to him was that he looked as if he'd never in his life have a wobbly moment.

She, on the other hand, had many wobbly moments. It wasn't that she was a pain, but she was a bit of a drama queen. So whatever went wrong for Kate, you knew about it. Work, the car, the house, the garden, the spaghetti bolognese down the white dress – Kate would have a wobble. And Steve would take the strain.

But Steve owns his own printing firm – and when one of his customers couldn't pay, and the whole operation took a nose dive, Kate did a mega-wobble. And three months to the day that he first came home and told her that they might lose everything, she wobbled back to her mother's and out of their marriage.

I hadn't known Kate well, but I was sad. Steve and I email each other regularly – just mates, as we've been for nearly thirty years since we met at college. And so I said I was sorry, and asked if there was anything I could do ...

In his next email, Steve started writing a little bit about what had been going on for him. Nothing revealing, just a few jokey sentences. I replied, as you do in emails, interspersing his paragraphs with supportive ones of my own.

In his next email, Steve wrote three paragraphs about how he'd felt. And the next contained twenty-two full paragraphs all about his money worries and how stressed out and insecure he was.

I was happy he felt he could let it all out. I was even happier when, as Steve continued to send the emails, they gradually became more and more positive. Until one day, he wrote to tell me that that he'd just been approached by a new investor, and that Kate wanted to come back. Wonderful, Steve.

Well, part wonderful. He'd said yes to the investor. And no to Kate. Why? His exact words were 'She always needed me to be there for her. But this time I fell apart – and she just wasn't there for me'.

Work problems, illness, family row, money worries, hassle with the kids – there are dozens of natural crises, big and small, that we'll all face at some time in our lives. And even the most solid of us get wobbly then. When we do get wobbly, that's when the support of our relationship becomes doubly important. That's when we most need to be accepted.

And if our relationship doesn't turn out to be a safe place, where what we feel can be accepted, it's a double betrayal. Kate left Steve not so much because there were money troubles, but because he fell apart emotionally and she couldn't handle that. Steve refused to have Kate back not just because she left him, but because she couldn't accept him when he fell apart.

When your partner is emotional – big time or small time – you need to provide extra safety. What will help him isn't only your acceptance of his problem, but also your acceptance of his feelings. What will help him is to know that with you at least, it's OK to wobble.

So first, be aware. Here are eight 'danger signals' your partner may use to try and tell you that he's feeling emotionally vulnerable:

- ♥ Being obviously down, silent, sad or tearful.
- ♥ Being obviously and untypically irritated or angry.
- ♥ Sleeping or eating more or less than usual.
- ♥ Wanting more or less sex than usual.
- ♥ Letting himself go, dressing badly, not shaving.
- ♥ Taking time off work or not wanting to work.
- ♥ Saying he feels down – though he may not know what's happening. 'I'm not feeling quite myself ... I feel very odd'.
- ♥ Seeming to want to talk – even if he isn't quite sure what he wants to talk about.

The next step is to help your partner realize that feeling emotional doesn't mean he's weak or a failure. As a man, he's almost certainly got this message from somewhere. But, if you can give him a different message and help him to see his feelings as completely natural and normal, then short-term he'll immediately feel better about himself. (And long-term he'll be more effective in the world because he knows he's OK even when he's feeling at his most vulnerable.)

So to start with, explain to your partner these four basic truths:

1 'Emotions are a real biological response to problems. In order to cope, your body prepares you for action by raising your heart beat, your blood pressure and your breathing. Adrenaline shoots round your body. No wonder you're feeling odd.'

2 'Anything even remotely threatening will trigger emotions, even if you're well prepared and able to cope. The fact that you're feeling emotional is a sign your body is reacting appropriately and preparing for action.'

3 'Expressing the emotion just a little, in words, is a way of

> reassuring your body that you've heard its signals to action and
> are doing something about them.'
> 4 'So by feeling the feelings, and talking about them you're actual-
> ly coping more effectively – not being soft.'

In terms of what to do next, it will work best to simply listen
if your partner wants to talk about his feelings. Notice that
word 'if' – he may not want to, and if he doesn't, that's fine.

If he does, don't even try to get him to stem the flow, by
distracting him or suggesting he cheers up – he'll just feel
sidetracked and not taken seriously. Instead, allow him to say
what he feels, to be anxious, to cry, to get angry. And be
patient if he wants to talk over things several times, to clear
them from his system – even if you've heard the story again
and again.

You can also help by asking questions to let him explore
things ... reflecting back what you're hearing so he can think
it through ... showing you understand with an occasional
nod, word, or touch.

And by continually reassuring him that he's not being
weak and wimpish – particularly if he says things such as
'Sorry ... I shouldn't be doing this ... you must think I've gone
mad ...'.

If you can do these things, your partner will almost always
recover from his painful emotions. He'll start thinking more
clearly, and coping more effectively. He'll gain energy and
motivation to start sorting out the problem.

Because what a partner needs is to know that however
wobbly he gets, you won't reject him.

And that when he's back on top, you'll love him just as
much as before.

Ps. This section of the book has been talking about manageable emotion, not unmanageable bad behaviour. If your partner's emotions lead him to drink, drugs, violence or self-harm, then the rules in this section don't apply because he's putting himself and others at risk.

In that case, don't hesitate. Ring one of the organizations mentioned in the back of the book and get support – for you first, and then for him.

Read this if you can't cope with his emotions

Have you seen those executive toys that were all the rage a few years back?

Silver balls on wires, hung from a horizontal rod. Let one ball fly and the return strike sends all the others ricocheting off each other in the same direction. And then back again in the opposite direction. Back again. And again. Constant movement triggered, one ball to the next, by a single initial strike.

It can happen in your relationship. If it does, it hurts.

Because if the two of you are close – particularly if you're very close – then any strong emotions that your partner feels will trigger a reaction in you. Not just a single reaction. But a string of reactions as one emotion sets the other off.

And often the ricochet effect triggers emotional memories too, so that horrors from the past come flying back into your mind, and make you feel even worse.

For example, when Emma had a big row with her ex as she was dropping the children off for their weekly visit, she did what she always does when she's got a problem. She went back home and told Tom. What she expected was sympathy and a listening ear.

What she got was an outburst about how she should have stood up for herself more.

Emma was shocked and hurt. She absolutely didn't need Tom to shout at her – she was already feeling bad enough. So eventually, with Tom still sounding off, she finished up her supper, took her dishes to the sink and went to bed. And Tom was left wondering what he'd said.

It might have all got forgotten, but the next week the whole thing blew up all over again, so once again she came back in tears. And when she did, needing desperately to talk about what was happening and how to handle it, Tom started all over again. Emma says that she had never, in their entire time together, felt nearer packing and walking out.

It was so unlike him not to be there for her. She couldn't believe it was Tom.

Luckily, that very thought stopped her in her tracks. And made her say 'Hold on a minute ... What's going on for you? Where are you in all this?' And then Tom stopped in his tracks, and started remembering.

Because Tom wasn't there with Emma, supporting her in what she was going through. He was way back in the past, ten years ago. His own marriage breakup, feeling completely blamed and scapegoated, but too scared of losing the kids to stand up for his rights. Angry at his ex-wife – angry too at himself for not being able to get what he needed. For Tom had just hung in there, let himself be trampled on – and had always regretted that.

And so of course he wasn't really listening to Emma's story. He was replaying his own story with its ten years of remembered pain.

No wonder he was finding it difficult to concentrate ...

When your partner is talking about something emotional – a big crisis or a tiny incident – you may find it difficult to concentrate too. You feel uncomfortable, you feel you can't cope with it – and you don't quite know why. What's happening is that you're living your partner's pain just too much. And all your past ghosts are living that pain too.

Not suprisingly, your angry or sad emotions erupt too, perhaps on your partner's behalf, perhaps even at him. Which not only makes him feel shouted at. It also doesn't allow him any shouting space for himself. You're too busy doing it for him.

Another variation may be this. You just can't handle all these raw emotions, and do whatever you can to get yourself or your partner feeling better. So you steer things away from the problem area, change the subject, get distracted, crack a joke – anything but really feel the feelings. Which means you partner not only doesn't get what he needs, because you're taking things in the opposite direction. He also gets the impression that you're not really interested in his problem at all.

Of course it's not easy. If your feelings are putting on this sort of performance, it's hard to let your partner's emotions take centre stage.

But at least for a while, do your best to stand in the wings. Keep your feelings silent and still. Accept your partner's feelings, so he can work them through – and get to the point where he can think clearly and make clear decisions.

Here are four useful things to tell yourself when what your partner's feeling is what you're feeling too:

♥ Adding my emotion to this problem won't help. It will just double my partner's burden.
♥ Feeling *with* my partner is supporting him. Feeling *instead* of my partner is just upstaging him.
♥ Wanting my partner to cheer up so *he'll* stop hurting is helpful. Wanting my partner to cheer up so *I'll* stop hurting is unhelpful.
♥ In a while, my partner's emotions will be satisfied. And then my emotions will get to have a turn.

Read this when your emotions run away with you

Often emotions are glorious. Sometimes, they're the last thing you need.

When you're supporting your partner and need to be really there for him ... when you're discussing something with your partner and need a clear head ... when you're arguing over something and want to separate the emotion from the issue you're trying to resolve ... in all those situations, the last thing you need is for your emotions to run away with you.

So here are four instant fixes:

♥ Breathe deeply – to relax your nervous system
♥ Distract yourself – take your attention from the feelings by saying your 'times table' or looking round the room
♥ Move about a bit – to burn off stressful adrenalin, take a brisk walk or jump up and down a few times – in the loo if it's not appropriate to do so in public!
♥ Take a break – at least twenty minutes on your own to allow the physiological sensations to fade and your body return to normal.

Breathe ... distract ... move ... take a break. Manage your emotions and you'll find it far easier to manage the situation.

Read this if he can't cope with your emotions

You deserve to feel.

You deserve to have a relationship where you can feel good – happy, euphoric, excited, motivated.

You also, actually, deserve to have a relationship where you can feel bad – upset, frustrated, angry. Because even those unhappy emotions are important, showing you when things are going wrong, alerting you to problems.

If your partner isn't a very emotional person, then this will directly affect how, and how much, you feel. Sometimes that's positive – if you're an 'up and down' sort of person, you'll probably be glad that your partner isn't; he'll pass on to you some of his emotional stability.

But if his lack of feeling is actually a lack of coping – if he backs off or freezes up every time you get weepy or moody – then this may be a problem.

If your partner can't cope with your feelings, then use these three strategies. When you get emotional:

Reassure him

Men aren't used to emotional displays. So a bout of tears, frustration or panic – which for you is par for the course – may make him think you're on the edge of breakdown. And that scares him because he cares for you.

In fact, given a few paper hankies and time to howl, you'll be fine. So tell him that. Explain that you'll soon stop feeling bad. If he learns you'll bounce back, he'll learn to bounce back too.

Give him something to do

A man likes to feel he's sorting things out, finding a solution to every problem – particularly when it's a problem that's affecting someone he loves. And the way he sees it, hanging in there while you howl isn't a solution.

You need to explain to him that hanging in there is a solution, in and of itself. He often doesn't need to do any more than hold you while you cry, or rant.

You could, also, ask your partner to do something specific for you – hold you, listen to you, pass the hankies. If he feels useful, he'll feel better.

Give him the goodies

If you want your partner to stick with it when you're feeling down, then when he does stick with it, reward him. Thank him, hug him, tell him he did well.

And, describe what he did and how it helped you. As a man, the idea of emotional coping may be a bit of a mystery to him – so say things like: 'When I was upset and you stayed and held my hand, that really helped me to calm down, and find a way out.'

If he understands why you're asking him to do what you're asking him to do, he'll be much more likely to be able to do it.

Simple truth about love

There are three secrets to building a wonderful emotional relationship:

Communication.

Communication.

And communication.

Read this if you suspect you talk more than you listen

Ian and I stop talking only in a sheer emergency.

When we were first going out we hardly slept because we were too busy gabbling, trying to make up for the inexplicable fact that we hadn't known each other all our lives. As we started to realize the relationship was serious, we both took on big projects at work, and spent most of our time usefully discussing how and when and exactly what we should do. I shudder to remember what our phone bill was like – British Telecom probably recorded record profits that year.

And then one day, I lost my job.

I stumbled round to Ian's flat in a daze, not quite believing what had happened, and certainly unable to cope with it. Ian cuddled me up and fed me warm drinks and did everything he could possibly think of to help.

Now, he's fiercely intelligent, always able to cut through the problem and come up with an answer. So for him, helping meant doing what he did best: thinking of solutions. What other jobs could I apply for? Who could I ring to tap into the job finder grapevine? Could I set up on my own? His words, and his love, spilled out over me in a comforting wave.

So why did I feel so uncomfortable?

Why did I feel like slapping my bright new boyfriend until he stopped bombarding me with words. Why did I just want to stop my ears and curl into a ball until he shut up?

By this time, he'd seen the look on my face, and slowly ground to a halt. Which gave me the chance to say – and yes, I do remember just how sarcastic I was being – 'Ian, why don't we swap roles. Just for a change, I'll do talking. And you do listening. OK?'

To do him credit, he didn't flinch. Just mentally stapled his lips together until I was done. An hour and several packets of paper hankies later, I'd decided to go freelance.

What I realized that day was that there are times in a relationship when what is needed is listening. Not making suggestions. Not exchanging horror stories. Not even asking questions – well at least until the first desperate layer of words has been creamed off.

Whether there's been an emergency or just a normal day at work, whether there's a decision to be made or some bad news to integrate, what both partners need is for the other to listen.

What I needed – and what I got, thank heaven, when Ian got the message – was space to say what I needed to say. To talk about what had happened so that I could express how upset and anxious I was. To explore what had happened with someone I knew was on my side, and who loved me.

And slowly, as I did all that, I could start to turn outward – to start making decisions that were right for me, to start taking action that I could carry through. But until Ian had listened to me, all I really wanted to do was howl.

You're probably thinking that you and your partner listen to each other all the time – over breakfast, doing the washing up, in front of the television at night. This is different – this is a special kind of listening. Not divided listening, with one eye on the clock or the kids. Or diluted listening, because you've got other things to do or other things on your mind.

This is the kind of listening which makes you each feel that just for a moment, you're the centre of attention. And because it makes you each feel that, it really, really helps.

Short-term, it lets you sort out problems more effectively. Long-term, it creates an opportunity within your relationship to explore your thoughts, feelings and possibilities – and so develop in a way that you've never done before.

So make time and space for listening to each other. Suggest it to your partner. Or simply listen to him a few times, let him find out how good it feels, and then ask for a return match. Listen at least once a day for at least five minutes each – more if something important needs talking through.

And as you listen, do your best to concentrate. Be quiet inside as well as out. Listen to what each other is saying,

love coach

without getting lost in your own thoughts, or rehearsing what you're going to say next.

Acknowledge. Give the message that you're listening, with an occasional nod, phrase or word of encouragement. You need to know you're with each other, all the way.

Notice what's really said. Get a real sense of what each other is communicating, verbally and nonverbally. What do the words tell you, between the lines? What does the body language show you, about what is or isn't being said?

Follow, rather than leading. Your thoughts, opinions and suggestions will have their turn. For just a few minutes, let the other take the conversation where they want without

having to take you into account.

Reflect. Repeating back what you think you've heard will help each of you check out whether you're on the right track. It will also make the other feel that what they're saying is been heard and acknowledged.

Stand back. Don't wade in with contradictions or arguments. Yes, of course if what one of you is saying is going to affect the other, then eventually there's got to be time for equal discussion and democratic decisions. But for the moment, give each other space to make their statement, their way.

And ask questions about what you're hearing. Not only to show you're interested, but also to give each other a chance to explore the issues. Questions open a door to new thoughts, new ideas and new possibilities.

Above all, when you're giving this sort of support, remember who's doing what.

Whoever's talking should do the talking.

Whoever's listening should do the listening.

Read this if he never talks to you

It's all very well suggesting that you communicate with your partner. But what if he won't talk?

It's a truism to say that men aren't as good at communicating as women. Yet it's still true. Yes, men get as much out of talking as women do – when they do it. But they often find it hard.

Usually, they've learned that it's hard. Your partner may feel you're the expert at communication, and that when he talks, it doesn't have the same effect.

Or he's been rubbished for what he's said. He's withdrawn into a shell of noncommunication because it feels safer.

If your partner doesn't find it easy to talk, particularly about what he feels or thinks, then use these three strategies.

♥ Realize the value of silence. Bombarding him with words of encouragement will typically only pressure him. Instead, talk less. He may take the opportunity to talk more.

♥ Learn to recognize when he does want to talk, when he needs attention, signals you don't recognize, such as long silences, or physical touch. So if he reaches out for you, fix the gaffer tape firmly over your own mouth.

♥ Make it a great experience for him to talk. Say how pleased you are that he's confided in you. Ask questions. Show you're interested. Make it worth his while to come out of his shell.

Read this if he never listens to you

It's all very well suggesting that you communicate with your partner. But what if he won't listen?

Bit of tough feedback coming up here. If your partner doesn't listen to you, it may be because you're talking so much that he's on overload.

Are you in the habit of talking most of the time, talking to fill silences, talking in a desperate attempt to get him to listen? If so, he may be shutting down because listening's painful.

Or it could be that your partner does pay attention, but doesn't show it in a way that makes you feel good. Men learn far fewer social signals than women do – and one of the gaps in their education is listening signals.

If your partner doesn't find it easy to listen, then use these three strategies:

♥ Teach him to use listening signals. Ask him specifically to acknowledge what you're saying with whatever signals make you feel heard – eye contact, a nod, a smile. Explain to him that these will help you feel understood.
♥ Get him to ask questions. Many men, brought up to think that what's expected of them is action, genuinely believe that doing their bit in a conversation means talking, rather than letting you talk. Explain to him that if he asks you questions and listens to your answers, you'll feel much more appreciated
♥ Give him credit for what he does do. Whenever he listens with interest, tell him and show him that you feel better afterwards. Make it worth his while to take the earplugs out permanently.

Read this if 'love' means different things to each of you

When Ian and I were in that early stage of learning all about each other, one of the things he told me was that he loved to be 'mothered'.

I knew about being mothered. My Mum was wonderful at it. It involved tomato soup, warm blankets, and lying on the sofa in front of the TV. It particularly came into its own when I was 'poorly', but it could swing into operation any time I was feeling a bit low.

So the first time Ian got flu', I knew exactly what to do. I propped him up with cushions, moved the television to a position where he could see it, started quizzing him on what sort of soup he liked.

He thought I'd gone completely off my head.

Because for Ian, 'mothering' was nothing to do with being ill, practical caring, or warm soup. For him, the word 'mothering' meant that during the course of daily life, he needed to be hugged a lot, and told he was getting it right. I'd been doing that – as a natural part of our relationship. But I hadn't realized that that was what he'd meant by 'mothering'.

And, I hadn't realized that when Ian was ill, the last thing he wanted was to be snuggled up with horrible nasty soup. What someone who loved him ought to do was leave him strictly alone, a wounded animal, until he felt better.

The lesson I learned that day was that if your partner tells you something, particularly about key concepts in your relationship, like 'love' or 'loyalty' or 'being faithful', you should never assume you know what he's on about.

Because some concepts in a relationship seem so obvious that we just assume that our partner has the same idea of what they are. They're part of the way we see the world, the way we expect the world should be. And because we expect the world 'should be' like that, we think it 'is' like that. And that our partner thinks it is like that too.

So we usually don't bother to spell out just what we mean ... and then we misunderstand each other ... and then we wonder why we're disappointing each other by not living up to expectations. By not delivering what we thought we'd agreed. By serving soup when what was really wanted was a large helping of hugs.

Talk through the key concepts in your relationship – even if you think that you know exactly what your partner means. Ask each other questions about these concepts. Check out the full meaning of them. Keep going until you're certain you understand.

Here are six key words that you'd do well to talk through with your partner:

♥ Honesty ... does it mean, for example, always telling the truth ... never telling a lie ... just speaking up when something's wrong?

♥ Freedom ... does it mean, for example, being able to say what you mean ... being able to spend time apart ... or being able to sleep with who you want?

♥ Commitment ... does it mean sexual faithfulness ... getting a mortgage together ... or having a child together?

♥ Loyalty ... does it mean not criticizing each other directly ... not criticizing each other to outsiders ... or hanging in there when things are bad?

♥ Fidelity ... does it mean not having other sexual relationships ... not having other emotional relationships ... or not even talking to a member of the opposite gender without permission?

♥ Love ... does it mean emotional connection ... sexual connection ... a strong feeling of affection ... or a lifelong promise to stay?

In the case of Ian and 'mothering', the solution was easy once we'd really understood.

Now when I'm ill, he moves in with the duvet and the tomato soup ...

When he's ill, I close the bedroom door and tiptoe quietly downstairs.

Read this when it's not the right time to talk

It's good to talk. But it's not always a good time to talk.

Because yes, you both need to communicate what you think and feel. To touch down at the end of the day. To troubleshoot in a crisis.

But there are times when doing that will just make things worse. Because you aren't in a state to communicate properly, or because the situation won't allow you to communicate properly.

Here are four occasions when it's best not to try talking things through with your partner because you just won't get a result:

♥ One or both of you is too tired. There's a myth that you should always stay up, get issues sorted before bed. But if you're too exhausted to think clearly – or so exhausted that you're bound to row – then leave it till the morning. Say 'I love you' then get a good night's sleep and come to it fresh.

♥ One or both of you is under the influence. Any substance that's mind-altering will also be communication-altering. You'll either fail to get your point across, fail to understand your partner's point, or end up screaming. Wait till you're both clearheaded and then talk.

♥ One of you is going away. It can seem essential to talk things through before you leave. But the very pressure of having to talk to a deadline can raise the desperation level. Instead, say clearly that you're committed to sorting things out. Then arrange a date and time when you'll definitely do that.

♥ There's a crisis. If work, family or kids have created an emergency, then you need to sort it. And you need to recognize that whoever's at the sharp edge of sorting it won't be able to concentrate on anything else for a while. After the crisis is over, you'll both have the time and focus to talk things through.

So yes, it's good to talk. But it's best to wait until you can do it properly.

Simple truth about love

When things get stressed, and seem out of control.

It's tempting to grab the steering wheel and hang on regardless.

That's great if you grab it together, and steer together.

But if you grab one way and he grabs the other ...

You're likely to cause an accident.

Read this if you like giving the orders

Don't you just love being in control?

There was an ad campaign with that tag line about six years ago, with a series of celebrities all grinning gleefully when they got what they wanted in life, courtesy of the power of a certain kind of fuel at their fingertips.

But it's true. We all like being in control. We have to be in control in order to survive. Control is one of those basic needs we all have. If we're helpless and dependent, then we're at real risk. We have to have some control over our environment to get food and warmth ... over other people so they don't do us down ... over our own reactions so they don't get out of hand. Natural, essential, no problem.

But when you're in a partnership, control is a problem.

Because if both of you want control, particularly if you want it in order to do different things, then you can think you need control over each other. And then, rather than working together as a team, to get control over your lives together, you turn it into a power struggle.

Here are six suspect ways that you or your partner might try to be in control:

- ♥ You give each other orders...
- ♥ You guilt trip each other...
- ♥ You block each other's ideas...
- ♥ You overdirect each other...
- ♥ You block each other's actions...
- ♥ You overrule each other's suggestions...

By now, you're probably thinking that anyone who does all that is a monster. And yes, if partners go in like that with all guns blazing all the time, then the war is quick and bloody and ends in the divorce court. (Or, perhaps even worse, as time passes one of you ends up ruling the roost and the other knuckles under for life.)

But for all that these controlling behaviours are outrageous, almost all of us do some quiet version of them at some time. We all slip them in when our partner doesn't notice – or even when we don't notice. And that's when the real harm's done.

It happened to a woman we'll call Leah. Her story will make you wince.

Leah went away for a long weekend, with her husband and two children, to one of those holiday villages. Lots of chalets hidden in the woods, with bicycle paths and a subtropical swimming paradise.

They had a great time – and every day they took their camcorder with them. The kids were particuarly keen, wanting film of themselves sailboarding, rollerskating and going down the flume in the subtropical paradise.

Back home, by Tuesday, with her husband working late and the kids in bed, Leah decided to review the video. Watched them all sailing on Friday, watched herself cooking supper in the chalet on Saturday. And then giggled as she realized that, during supper and afterwards, someone had left the video on the sofa, still running.

The view was uninspiring – straight across the room at knee level, catching table and chair legs along the way. But as Leah let the film run, at any minute intending to fast forward, she found herself transfixed by the sound track.

And she didn't like it one little bit.

love coach

For a start, the tone of voice she used to her husband was horribly similar to the one she used to her eight-year-old. And the words she used to her husband weren't much different either. She hadn't realized that her main interaction with him was to tell him what he shouldn't be doing. Or that her main single word to him was 'No'.

And she hadn't realized just quite how flat and emotionless his voice was as he spoke back to her. When he spoke back to her. Which he didn't, much.

In the hour Leah had before her husband came back home, she did a lot of thinking. And from what she says, a lot of changing. When he came home, she gave him the biggest hug they'd had in ages – and from then on, started mentally editing everything she said and did to treat him like a partner, not a subordinate.

They're still together, two years on, and unrecognizably happier. Would they have still been together if the camcorder had been turned off? Leah reckons not.

If you have a horrible feeling that a video clip of your relationship would be just as damning to you as it was to Leah, then the illustrations show you some things you can change.

Read this if you're scared of surrendering control

If you tend the lead in how your relationship is run, then even the very idea of not doing that may make you feel surprisingly uncomfortable.

Because it can literally make you feel 'out of control'. And that's frightening. Here are some fears you may have:

'I'm scared of being gagged'

You may feel that if you hold back to allow your partner more input into what's happening, you'll never get a say over anything. Not true. Sharing control doesn't mean not inputting ideas at all. It means inputting them in a way that gives your partner space to input too – and then lets you both talk things through and then start to work as a team.

'I'm scared of being taken over'

If you back off and let go of control, at first your partner may rush in and try to make all the decisions. But when he realizes that he needn't fight you in order to get any control at all, he'll ease off and you'll get a more equal balance of power. Teach your partner how to cooperate in the relationship by cooperating yourself.

'I'm scared of problems'

If you pull back on instructing and directing your partner, he may mess up – he's probably starting to do things and make decisions he hasn't done before. Don't jump in and don't gloat. Instead be there when he gets it wrong so that he can talk it through and learn.

'I'm scared of disaster'

Some controls on a relationship seem crucial – not to have an affair ... not to get drunk every night ... not to be violent or abusive. And if your partner normally does these sorts of bad behaviour, then discuss it, sort it or get out. But if he doesn't normally do these things, then he won't start just because you're not policing him.

'I'm scared of giving up all control'

Of course, there's no place in love for giving up all control. If you do it and end up feeling that you're submitting ... or surrendering ... or having to be subservient ... then there's something very wrong.

But if you feel that what's most important in your relationship is to be in control of everything, then actually there's something wrong with that too.

So be honest with yourself. Do you need to lose a little control to put your relationship on an equal basis? If so, do it.

Because if you don't lose just a little, eventually you'll lose the lot.

Lose your partner. Lose your relationship. Lose your love.

Read this if he keeps running power trips

If you suspect your partner's trying to take control in your relationship, then you're probably right.

Because needing to be in control is natural. So even if only a little, your partner almost certainly wants things to go his way.

But if he wants to take too much control, you do need to challenge it.

We're not talking here about times when it's appropriate for him to take charge – like when he's the one who's driving. Or times when expertise needs to take precedence – like when he's the one who knows the recipe.

And we're not talking about the times when you both want your own way, but in fact it's a fair fight. Or, of course, the times when you'll happily give up what you want so that you can both get on with loving each other.

But when your partner takes control compulsively ... or always ... or in everything important ... or on every tiny thing ... or at the expense of your sanity ... then your relationship is out of balance. And something needs to change.

Though actually that something has to be you.

Because though your partner's control patterns are not your fault, they are your problem. Your partner isn't going to suddenly reform. Why should he when he doesn't realize that what he's doing is causing a problem – and if he does realize, when he thinks that the way to avoid problems is to take even tighter control?

However ... remember that you're the one who has the

possibility here to change what is happening – because you're the one who understands what is happening. It may mean acting firmly, or even making waves – and that may be so hard to achieve that in the end you decide not to bother. But if you choose to, then almost always you can do it.

Here are six things you'll have to do if you want to shift the balance of power in your relationship:

♥ Be certain of what you want. If you're unsteady, your partner will naturally tilt the control in his direction. If you are certain and communicate that clearly, he'll find taking the reins much more difficult.

♥ Be certain of what you don't want. Unless you set limits, your partner will break them without even realizing it. If you set your boundaries, then you'll find it easier to keep him at bay.

♥ Be calm about what you want. If you get angry and push, your partner will only push back harder. If you stay flexible, he'll find it much more difficult to tilt you over.

♥ Be energetic about what you want. If you get upset and collapse, your partner may overwhelm you. If you stand firm, he'll find it much more difficult to unbalance you.

♥ Be patient. When you first challenge your partner's control patterns, he'll react strongly and negatively. He'll try to convince you that you're acting unwisely, unawarely or unlovingly. Hang in there.

♥ Decide on your bottom line. If your partner refuses to share control, what then? What will you do? Unless you know when to say 'enough', then he'll always be able to call your bluff and he'll keep on running his power trips.

Read this when you both try to take charge

It had been a wonderful day up to then.

We'd met, the six of us, on the towpath early that morning and walked along to the narrowboat. After a flurry of preparations, we'd glided slowly away from the moorings and set off down to Bath. A five-hour journey. And nothing much else to do but laze in the sunshine.

Tim and Jane owned the boat. But they were totally up for everyone to lend a hand, and so we each took turns at the tiller for a mile or two and then changed places. Until just before the woods, with Sean steering, another boat came round the bend towards us, far too fast and with a bow wave.

What Tim should have done – as the most experienced there – was jump down from the boat roof and take the steering back. What he actually did was to call instructions, at first calmly and then with increasing urgency.

As the two boats neared, Jane panicked, and we all shouted too – but by this time, Sean was beyond hearing, and everyone's advice only confused him. And when the crew of the other boat and all the people on the towpath joined in, Sean lost it completely.

Then all voices fell silent as steel hit steel with a body-wrenching crash ...

Most of the time, it's right and fair and effective in a partnership to discuss everything and make decisions together. Sometimes it's the way to total disaster.

If you're in an emergency and things need deciding quickly

... if one of you has real expertise that rightly pulls rank. ... if a project needs a single clear vision rather than a lot of different varied inputs ... then you'll do much better if only one partner takes charge and the other follows.

Isn't that over-traditional and politically incorrect? Am I saying 'he' should make all the decisions and 'she' should follow on? Absolutely not. But in some situations, for a set time or in a set context, one of you should make the decisions and take the responsibility, and the other should stand well clear.

Sometimes that other will be your partner – in which case, he needs to let you get on with the job. And if he won't, you need to tell him to back off.

But sometimes, that other will be you. And if it is, then you should back off. Don't try to take over, even if it's blindingly obvious you'd do a better job; or give advice, even if you know your advice is sound; or stand on the towpath and make critical comments, even if something's going very wrong.

Instead, respect your partner's vision so that he can develop it and make things happen. Give enthusiastic support because being in charge isn't an easy job. Help him think things through – in his way not yours, with questions rather than suggestions, and appreciations rather than criticisms.

These ten phrases will be useful at times when you're standing well clear:

♥ What are you aiming to do?
♥ What do you need to consider?
♥ How do you need to tackle this?
♥ What are the problems here?
♥ What else do you need in order to do that?

- ♥ How could you get round what's stopping you?
- ♥ Who or what could help you?
- ♥ What do you need me to do now?
- ♥ What should I not do?
- ♥ or simply ... How can I help?

This strategy will work on small issues – where one of you is cooking the dinner and the other isn't. It will work on big issues – where one of you is trying to cope with a work project and the other isn't.

It won't work where both of you have equal responsibility and need to act as a unified team – such as bringing up your kids. And it needs to be handled carefully and with consultation when a decision's being made that's going to affect everyone deeply – such as whether to relocate.

But it will work where such a decision has been made but the different bits of implementing the decision – like how to organize the packing cases – are more easily organized by each of you taking one area of responsibility and making it happen alone.

Because what it boils down to is this. There are times in your relationship when actually, it works much better if just one of you steers the boat.

Read this when you're tempted to muscle in

When you're partners, it's very easy to think that every single thing the other does is laid out for your inspection, your comment, your input.

But in fact, everyone needs some things in their life that are theirs and theirs alone. Maybe their job. Maybe their hobbies. Maybe what they wear. Maybe the friends they hang out with.

If your partner has something central to his life that's very dear to him, by all means be interested. But hold back from commenting, inputting, criticizing – from anything that tries to get him to do it your way.

Some things your partner thinks, feels, says and does are his – his to work out, his to explore, his to enjoy.

Some things about your partner are, quite literally, none of your business.

Simple truth about love

Love can seem like a tug of war. He wants control. You want control. He wants what he needs. You want what you need.

Loop the rope round what you both need and start tugging together. With two of you pulling, you'll get what you need twice as fast.

And with half the effort.

love coach

Read this if you're feeling disappointed

Almost certainly, when you were little, there was a grown-up around who was on your side. It was probably your Mum, though it might have been your Dad or another important adult.

If you were frightened of the dark, your Mum or Dad cuddled you up and kept you safe.

If the girl who sat behind you in class told you you were horrible, your Mum or Dad told you you were wonderful.

If you felt everything was too difficult, your Mum or Dad helped you get on top of it, cope with it, be in control of it.

Of course, being human, your parents couldn't do all these things for you completely, or all the time. But in general, when there was a problem, they were there for you.

When you're in a relationship, what you want isn't just the hearts and flowers, the bright lights and the excitement. What you want, deep down, is your Mum and Dad back. You don't literally want to be a child again. But you do want to have on tap those feelings of being safe, OK and generally in control of things that your parents gave you.

Of course, your partner will do his best to oblige. And particularly at the start of the relationship, when everything's exciting and fresh, it will seem as if he's delivering.

But in the end, he just won't be able to. He can't always protect you from everything (it's a cruel world out there). He can't always tell you you're utterly wonderful (sometimes he'll think you're not). And he won't always let you be in control of everything (he wants a say in things too).

The hard truth is this: If you expect your partner to make you feel completely safe, completely OK, and completely on top of everything in your life, then you're going to be disappointed.

And if you're starting to feel disappointed in your relationship at the moment, it's probably because you're expecting your partner to make you feel completely safe, completely OK and completely on top of everything

If you haven't realized it before, then realize it now. Sadly, your partner can't do everything for you.

Because your partner isn't your Mother

Your partner isn't your Father

Your partner isn't God ...

Read this when you find that giving's not easy

Of course you have day to day needs in life. So does your partner. And if you really love each other, then you'll meet each other's needs completely and effortlessly.

Won't you?

That's certainly the way successful love is said to work. The media hype – from Middle Ages' romantic ballads right the way through to Millennium top ten hits – tells us that love is about two people meeting each other's lifelong needs. Without struggle. Without trouble. Without pain.

It's a myth.

Yes in the glorious early days it will feel as if you can give and give – anything and everything – just because you love each other. But later on, what you're being asked to give may not be what you want to give. And then having to love may begin to bite.

The media hype never mentions that fact. It sells the idea that in a perfect relationship, you will want to give to your partner completely and he will want to give to you. And that if you don't, then your relationship is much less than perfect – it's probably not even the right relationship for you.

And so when – as always happens – you realize that giving's not easy, you'll probably panic.

Here's the truth that explodes the myth.

Even if you love each other to bits, the fact that you're different people will mean you want and need different things. That's natural, a fact of life, not your fault. This will particularly happen as your relationship develops, and as you develop in different ways.

Because there will be clashes. He'll want you to give him sex and you'll feel tired, to give him support and you'll feel resentful. Or you'll want him to give you a back massage and he'll be too busy, to give you a baby and he'll back off across the room.

These situations are never easy, so don't think they will be. It will sometimes hurt to give something to your partner, or to give up something for your partner's sake. It will sometimes hurt your partner when you don't give up something for his sake. And it will sometimes hurt you when you realize that your partner isn't going to give up everything for your sake – and then has the gall to tell you he still loves you!

The bottom line is that even in the happiest and most successful of relationships, you'll have to balance out your needs and your partner's needs.

And you'll have to do that every day for the rest of your life.

Read this if you wonder why you should bother giving

Why do it? Why bother giving – or giving up – a single thing for love? The answer's pragmatic as well as romantic.

Because the basic bargain is this. Giving is the price of a loving relationship. Like any financial settlement, you largely get out what you put in.

Here are the three main paybacks you'll get from giving:

♥ If you give to your partner, then short-term he'll be more motivated to return the favour.
♥ If you give to your partner, then medium-term you'll create a climate where you'll both learn to give more to each other and so will get more from each other.
♥ If you give to your partner, then long-term you'll avoid the natural tendency of every relationship, over time, to turn into two individuals only looking out for themselves.

Ps. Not always, of course. Sometimes you'll get your heart broken. But if you don't do the giving that is at the core of loving, then you'll never get to the point where hearts are involved at all ...

Read this if you're tempted to give too much

Meg found out just how much John loved her because of a pair of skis.

They'd been out just three times, had talked and talked, had laughed and laughed. And by the end of the third evening they were together, both of them knew that this was something very special.

The fourth evening, John invited Meg back to his flat. In through the door, he went ahead to the kitchen, calling back over his shoulder 'Just hang your coat up'. So Meg slipped her coat off her shoulders, and opened the closet door.

There, shining and bright, were a pair of long, slim, professional snow skis. And Meg's stomach turned over.

Because she hated skiing, hated the experience of it (which she'd tried, once), hated the thought of it (even from afar, it made her tremble with fear). And she was suddenly very afraid that, if this wonderful, fascinating man she'd just met loved skiing just half as much as those perfectly waxed and obviously expensive skis suggested he did, then she and he had more or less no chance of a working, living, loving future together.

She took a deep breath. And turned, to find John watching her. She said, carefully 'Do you ski, then?'

John looked at her face. He looked at the skis. And he thought of the unique experience of skiing the perfect run, as he'd been doing every winter for the best part of his adult life. And he said,

'Not necessarily'.

They were married in the spring eight months later. And John never skiied again.

It is, wouldn't you say, a wonderfully romantic story? It is, wouldn't you agree, the perfect expression of what sacrifice one person can make for another, an ultimate expression of love?

Well, not necessarily.

Yes, John saw that his skiing was a potential barrier between him and Meg. And that to lay it aside was a simple and foolproof way to avoid any possibility of conflict or hurt.

But it wasn't, necessarily, the best way to have a lifelong relationship that worked well for both of them.

Because though love is an endless series of small sacrifices, when it involves a big sacrifice of a vital part of your life, you're laying down problems for yourself. If in order to make the relationship work, you or your partner give up something that means almost everything to you, then you put your relationship under a pressure which may be almost intolerable.

Or completely intolerable, so the relationship cracks.

If you know that something in your life or your partner's life is very precious and yet isn't being included in your relationship, face that. Sit down and talk it through. Be understanding, tolerant, clear about what you each need and creative in your mutual solutions. Together, find some way that you can include that precious thing in your love, rather than excluding it. And remember that you deserve to follow your heart.

Because thirty years later, John has never once used his skis. And that's a real sign of his love for Meg.

And I'm not saying that Meg should have let him carry on skiing regardless of her feelings, as a real sign of her love for him.

But wouldn't it have been lovely if they'd have found a way to let John carry on skiing and Meg be genuinely happy about it?

Now, that would have been a real sign of love triumphant.

Read this if your relationship doesn't meet your every need

Some time in the early twentieth century, the City of York decided to introduce double-decker buses. York's a medieval city, with wonderful stone walls all round, broken only by medieval arches spanning all the roads into the town.

Now, a standard double-decker bus, as you might expect, has square corners. The arches through York City Walls are pointed.

The City Council gulped at the problem.

They found a solution though. The arches stayed. It was the buses that got altered. Quite simply, they were made to fit. They built them with pointed tops.

It's like that with love a lot of the time. Your partner gives you rock-solid emotional security – but is absolutely not up for that round-the-world trip you've always wanted. Or the relationship is fabulous in bed and out of it – but money is in short supply and looks like it always will be.

On a practical level, you have the full set – almost. You're getting what you want from your partner – nearly. But you're never quite sure whether that's good enough.

Of course, if what's happening doesn't fulfil your most fundamental needs – for respect, support, loyalty – then it's not good enough. And you shouldn't even try to slot the pieces together.

But if you know your love is basically good, but there are just a few things that don't seem to fit, then do this:

Stop asking for the impossible.

Instead, accept the possible and make it work.

♥ Get clear what needs your partner absolutely has to meet in order to stay your partner. (And make sure he knows too.)

♥ But be prepared to adapt your needs and give up wanting some things. (That isn't surrender, it's love.)

♥ Meet some of your needs with friends, family, workmates. (It doesn't mean you're being disloyal.)

♥ Accept that your partner has to meet some of his needs with friends, family, workmates. (It doesn't mean you're not enough for him.)

♥ Learn ways of telling each other what your needs are, and then commit to meeting them. (Being clear about needs doesn't mean being unromantic.)

♥ Work out what needs your partner can't meet and either accept that, or leave. (It isn't fair to blame him for what you know he can't deliver.)

♥ Find out what needs you have to meet in order to keep your partner happy. Then meet them. Or let him leave.

Read this if you can't always get what you want

My goddaughter Ellie is nine now, and a total tomboy. Best footballer in her class, no slide is too high for her – and when Ellie wants something, she really goes for it, with everything she's got.

But sometimes, that's her problem.

Last Christmas, among Ellie's presents was a beautiful Chinese puzzle – you probably know the sort, a box made of carved wood with all the bits fitting one into the other, so that you just can't see how it opens. It was, I have to say, not the right present for a nine-year-old at all. But some retired uncle had seen it and fallen in love with it and thought that Ellie would like it.

What he didn't think was that Ellie would try to open it without bothering to find out how.

Her eyes went wide as she took it out of the wrapping. All that wonderful, complex carving. She tried to lift the lid, couldn't, got told 'there's a secret to it ...' – and then in a flurry of wrapping paper she went on to the next present. A little while later, I saw her trying to shake the box open, then trying to twist it open.

What I didn't see was her taking it into the kitchen and launching a full scale attack.

But when I was clearing up after Christmas lunch, I took some dishes to the sink, and found the Chinese box on the floor. Scratched. Scraped. Probably jumped on. Ellie hadn't managed to open the box. But she had scarred it for life.

As she saw me looking at it, she came over and knelt beside me. She knew what she'd done. And as I delicately eased the vital wooden piece out of its hidden slot and lifted the lid of the box gently open, Ellie looked at me and grimaced. Too right, Ellie. Too right.

Sometimes getting what we need from a partner is a bit like trying to open the Chinese box. We want something small like a hug or help with the ironing. We want something big like support with a work problem or agreement to buy a car. We can't see how to get these things. We feel frustrated and irritated and probably also helpless. So in our frustration, we end up trying stunts that aren't useful.

Like Ellie, we absolutely don't mean any harm. But in the end, we do damage.

These six strategies feel tempting at the time:

♥ A big explosion – causing a fuss with anger or tears. In the end, your partner strikes back out of rage.
♥ War of attrition – nagging or reminding. In the end your partner shuts off out of resentment.
♥ Dictator style – ordering, commanding, telling him. In the end your partner rebels out of desperation.
♥ Playing victim – seeming helpless, appealing to his chivalry. In the end your partner stops supporting you, out of weariness.
♥ The con job – simply lying to get what you want. In the end your partner pulls back out of disillusionment.
♥ Not delivering – withholding attention or words or sex until you get what you want. In the end your partner withholds too, out of revenge.

These things may get you what you need here and now. But over time, they're going to scar any relationship – in time one or both of you will get battered by the demands or expert at digging your heels in.

Yet what's the alternative? How can you get what you need? The answer is often as straightforward yet as subtle as that hidden piece of wood. Try asking.

Ask clearly. You may be tempted to think that if your partner loves you, that means that he should know what you want. But, however close a couple is, partners aren't mind-readers. If you say clearly what you need, make a direct suggestion, you've got a much better chance of getting it.

Ask in positives. If you ask your partner 'not to do' something, you're setting up problems because you're not making it clear just what you do want. So he won't know what to deliver. He's more likely to do what you want if you say positively what that is.

Ask with understanding. You've got every right to suggest what you want in your relationship. But bear in mind that your partner has every right to have reservations about your suggestion. So be aware of his point of view as you do your asking.

Ask in a way that persuades. Head up your suggestion with reasons why it's a good idea, reasons that you've thought through, reasons that your partner can believe in too. Often the best persuader is simply 'I'd love it if you'd ...' or 'It'd make me really happy if ...'. This isn't manipulation, it's motivation – you're giving him a way to be happy by making you happy.

Ask with options. Have some alternatives in mind that you can talk through with your partner rather than just presenting him with one option and a 'yes ... no' choice. That will give him more room to get the result that he wants as well as the one you want.

Ask with time-awareness. Often your partner needs an

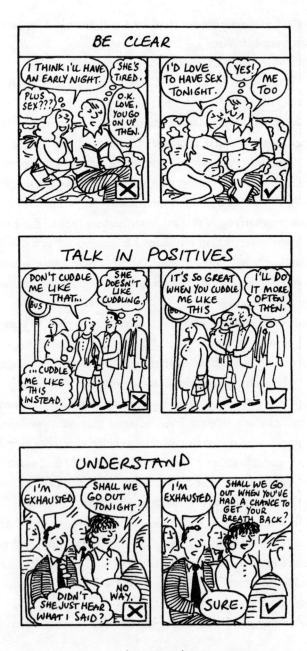

love coach

opportunity to think, to consider the pros and cons of your suggestion – or simply to be in a state to get his head round what you're proposing. If you demand an instant response you're likely to get an instant maybe, or an instant block. If you allow time and space for thought, then what you'll get back will typically be a more flexible response.

As always, if you can develop this skill, it will dripfeed positively through the rest of your relationship. Learn to ask, and your partner won't just be more inclined to say 'yes' to you. He'll also be more motivated to ask you things in a way that lets you say 'yes'.

Read this when he says 'no' to you

So you ask your partner for something. Or to do something. Something small like getting the milk, something big like getting a new job.

He says 'no'.

Or he says 'yes' and then doesn't deliver. Or he says 'yes' and you suspect he means 'no' and is just scared of the repercussions. Or he says 'maybe' and that always means 'no'.

It's hard, at this point, to simply stand back and let it go. You want something and you're not getting it. And on top of that frustration there's a slow-burning realization that the person who's stopping you getting what you want is the person who's supposed to love you.

Here are five possible reasons why your partner might say 'no' – and some useful ways to respond to each:

If your partner's saying 'no' because he thinks it's a bad idea

There may be very good and logical reasons why your partner doesn't agree with what you're asking. There may be unremoveable barriers, or undeniable blocks.

So find out what these are. 'Can we talk about your reasons ...', 'Tell me the problem with that ...'. It could be your partner's correct and your suggestion's a bad idea. It could be you're correct and that if you give yourself the chance to explain it more fully, he'll change his mind.

If your partner is saying 'no' because he wants things a different way

Your partner may want what you want, but differently from how you've suggested – with different people, or a different timing, or a different location. So if you want something, and he's holding back, don't assume that's a 'no'. It might be a '"yes", but not like that ...'

Again, ask questions to explore his issues and resolve them: 'What do you need to do in order to go ahead?' 'What needs to be different for you to be happy?'.

If your partner is saying 'no' just to hurt you

If you really think this is true, then are you in the right relationship? If things have got to a point where one of you is refusing out of viciousness, then you deserve better.

If your partner is saying 'no' because he doesn't feel able to do what you want

Often, your partner says 'no' not because he won't but because he feels he can't – he hasn't the slightest idea how to start. He can't see a way to get the resources needed – time, energy, skill.

Good questions will help him realize that it's possible to get those resources – 'So how could we do that?' 'What can I do to help you?' 'Would it work if we?'.

Your partner is saying 'no' because he's scared of failing

A variation on a theme is that your partner's wary of even trying what you suggest in case he gets it wrong. Often he's actually scared he'll let you down or look like a fool in front of you.

So tell him that if he tries and things don't work out, you won't be angry. Then talk him through step by step what needs to happen, and how he can gain confidence to give things a go.

Because actually, if you can find out what your partner's problems are, and make it clear that you're going to help overcome those problems, you'll probably be able to come up with solutions.

And then he'll come up with the goods.

Simple truth about love

The most wonderful words you've ever said to each other are probably 'I love you.'

The most scary words you've ever said to each other are probably 'I really need you to' and 'I really *do not* need you to ...'.

It's easy to love when you're being asked to feel.

It's hard to love when you're being asked to deliver, to provide, to adapt, to change.

Read this when you want him to change

There's an old saying that goes something like this: 'A man marries a woman thinking that she'll remain the same for ever. A woman marries a man thinking that she can change him.'

There will be times in your life when you want to change your partner. Little things about him bug you. Big things drive you up the wall. Of course you deserve the partner you want and the relationship you want – but you also need to take reality into account. And in reality, there are three possible outcomes.

Some things about him will never change

Your partner's deep-level personality ... his talents. ... his sexual preferences ... some things he does or says or believes ... are so much part of his nature and so important to his identity that they'll almost certainly never change.

So don't even try. Learn to live with them – and if you really can't, learn to live without him.

Some things about him will change of their own accord, given time and maturity

The laugh-a-minute guy in his early twenties may – if his attitude is down to youth and the people he hangs out with – become a responsible sober citizen in his early thirties.

Don't bank on it. But everyone changes, automatically, because of their life experiences, the people they meet, the things they do. So if the something that bugs you seems to be linked with his stage in life, waiting it out may sort it out.

Some things about him will change because of what you do

Some things about your partner you have control over, but not in the way you probably think.

Your partner won't change if you nag him, or blame him, or throw a tantrum every time he errs. He'll either dig his heels in, or he'll seem to toe the line but dig his heels in secretly.

In fact, the fact that you're nagging, blaming, and tantrumming will mean he does things more – not intentionally, but just because human beings tend to do more of what they get attention for, even if that attention is negative rather than positive.

But your partner will change if he wants to, and if you support him to. And if he does want to, and you do want to support him, then these four guidelines – adapted from an Army Teaching Manual – will help:

♥ If you tell your partner what you want him to do, he'll mysteriously forget.

♥ If you show him what you want him to do – by doing it yourself, for his benefit – then he'll start to understand why you're asking.

♥ If he does it for you – even just one time – he'll remember.

♥ If you show him that by doing it for you he makes you really happy, he'll do it for ever.

Read this when you want to change and he wobbles

There's an old saying that goes something like this. 'A woman marries a man thinking that she can change him. A man marries a woman thinking that she'll remain the same for ever.'

There will be times in your life when you want to change things for yourself. You'll want to take that course, apply for that job, lose that weight. These changes may well be completely positive for you, a sign you're moving on.

But they won't only change you – through you they'll change your relationship and your whole life together. And because of that, though you deserve to develop in any way you want, you need to take into account your partner's reaction too. There are three possible ways he might react:

He's really happy

Great. Go for it. But don't forget to involve him in what's happening. Share your enthusiasms and triumphs so that he gets the goodies of seeing his support make your change work.

He's happy in theory

He thinks what you want to do is a great idea. But you suspect that when it happens, he won't be quite so happy. The practical implications will bug him, because you're around less or he has to do more. Or the emotional implications will bother him, because he'll feel insecure or sidelined.

The answer is to talk through any potential downsides with your partner ahead of time, make sure he knows what may go wrong – and how you can both work to put it right. If he knows the solutions, he'll be much less wobbled by the problems.

He's really unhappy

If your partner is actively blocking a change you want to make in your life you have a three-way choice. Either give up your change completely. Or go ahead and do it anyway. Or negotiate so that what you do is acceptable to both of you.

♥ Option one will make you resentful and unhappy, now and in the future.

♥ Option two will make him resentful and unhappy now and in the future.

♥ If you're still committed to your relationship, only option three is really viable. Look at page 124 for guidance on how to make it work.

Read this when he wants you to change

Here's how to save a wedding anniversary from disaster. In one very tough lesson.

They'd been out for a fabulous meal – back to the actual hotel where they married seven years before. The setting was wonderful, the food to die for, the manager remembered them and brought over a complimentary glass of champagne. Everything was soft focus and romantic. Until it came to dessert.

He ordered something sweet, sticky and hugely calorific. She, counting the calories, didn't order one for herself, but asked for an extra spoon. Yes, she noticed his wince as she did it, but the waitress laughed and brought the two spoons, and they got stuck in.

She'd eaten about a third of what was on his plate before he said, ruefully, 'What stopped you ordering a dessert of your own? Then, just possibly, I could have had some of mine.'

She felt rage rush over her. Why on earth was such a wonderful evening about to turn into a flaming row? Then she took a deep breath and said 'OK, what would you have liked me to do?'.

He told her, and she listened. He didn't go on endlessly – it was a tiny thing. But he had felt forced to share. He needed to have a whole pudding to himself now and again. More than that, he needed her to understand that that was what he needed. Just a few sentences, and he thanked her and said he was feeling better.

She was feeling better too.

It wasn't just that they'd avoided a row. It was that they'd found a new way to cope with problems. He'd put up a flag about what he needed, and rather than jumping down his throat, she'd taken him seriously and taken what he said on board. The difference was huge.

One of the big contrasts between relationships that work and relationships that don't work is whether you can both say what you don't want as well as what you do want – and then do something about it.

Of course that's hard. It's really hard to listen to your partner telling you what he finds a problem, what he doesn't like, what he doesn't need. It's hard to hear 'It really bugs me when ... can you do this differently ... can you stop doing that ...'.

It can feel like you're being criticized, being told to change. And you are.

And that's tough. But all relationships have times when what one partner is doing drives the other to the edge. And you need a way of sorting those times.

So if your partner asks you to do something, pay attention. Make it clear that you're taking it seriously. That way, he'll be more likely to take you seriously when you say what you don't like.

And be open rather than defensive. Of course what you're doing isn't wrong or evil, and your partner should never tell you it is. But what you're doing is pushing your partner's buttons – and that's a good reason to stop.

Avoid counterattack – it rarely works. Of course your partner does things that bug you too – but that's no reason not to sort the things that bug him. Take what he's saying on board, and take responsibility for changing it.

And avoid listening to what your partner is saying, then doing nothing. Yes, discuss solutions that suit you both, and negotiate until you're both happy. But your partner's cry for help is also a call for action.

All this may feel very dangerous. Women in particular have had such a rough deal in matters of equality that being willing to change may feel just too much like being willing to grovel. These are some of the objections you may come up with when you think about altering what you do to meet your partner's needs.

'Give me a break! I can't remember him adapting to please me!'

If your partner has actually never listened to any of your requests, or if he compulsively blocks things just because you want them, then he's a serious power junkie and you should be careful.

But typically, it's only in the heat of total fury that we imagine partners never reciprocate. When we cool down, we remember loads of times they were kind and generous and giving.

In any case, like most of the strategies in the book, this one's aimed at getting both of you to change what you do. So the goal isn't that you adapt and he doesn't. It's that by setting an example, you get both of you adapting to please the other.

'I'm wary that if I start changing when my partner asks, then he'll start demanding I change completely what I think, feel and do.'

There's a real fear that saying 'yes' to a partner over some things will mean saying 'yes' to him over everything. But it doesn't actually work like that in practice.

In practice, almost always what he wants is something small, a shift in your approach rather than a major revamp, a willingness to stop and think rather than a whole personality change.

So of course if what your partner asks of you is against your principles, stand firm. But if he's asking you to do something that you can do, then at least try to do it. You may find that just a tiny shift in you makes a huge difference for him.

'If I show willing when my partner has a go at me, won't he just learn that having a go at me is the way to control me?'

If you jump to attention every time your partner clicks his fingers, then yes, he'll do it more. And if he's backing his requests up by bullying, pressuring, or by any sort of emotional blackmail, then you need to say a clear and unequivocal 'no'. But we're not talking about that. We're talking about listening when he has a complaint, so that short-term he'll feel taken seriously, more relaxed, more loved.

And so that long-term he'll feel more confident that problems will get sorted. Be a lot more laid back about minor irritations. And be a lot more up for returning the favour and listening when you have a complaint.

With both of you doing that, your relationship will have a self-repair mechanism. Quite simply, over time you'll both get less and less of what you don't want, and more and more of what you do want.

Read this when what you're offering isn't what he wants

Simon had a real problem with his Mum. It doesn't actually matter what the problem was. What matters is that his partner Nicola couldn't help him.

She tried just listening; he needed suggestions. She made suggestions; they weren't quite right. 'You're not helping,' said Simon. Nicola knew that. As the days went by, and Simon still struggled with his problem, she alternately felt bad about herself and furious with him. But nothing she said or didn't say made any difference.

One evening, when they'd been talking far too long and far too late, Nicola finally found the magic words. Because in sheer desperation, she turned to Simon and said:

'Well ... well ... for heaven's sake, what do you want me to say?'.

He told her what he wanted her to say. He'd known all along, though he hadn't known he'd known. But when Nicola asked Simon what he needed, some part of him was able to tell her just the questions to ask that let him think through the problem, feel better, and solve it.

So often, we want to meet a partner's needs, in tiny ways and in big ways. We offer a suggestion, a word, a touch. And what we're offering is the best thing we know how to offer – it's what works for us.

What we don't realize is that what works for us isn't necessarily what works for our partner. He's different – and so he has different needs. Then he gets irritated and frustrated because he's not getting what's helpful. And we get irritated and frustrated because we can't seem to help.

So next time your partner's struggling with life ... and you try to help him ... and he just doesn't want what you're offering, hold back from your tried and tested solutions, and hold back on the frustration that he doesn't want your tried and tested solutions.

Instead, ask: 'What do you need me to do? What do you need me to say? What do you need?'.

Your partner may need words. He may need silence. He may need distracting. He may need a cuddle. He may need leaving completely alone. He may need something entirely practical like a cup of tea. He may need something completely emotional, like permission to howl.

Go with it if you can.

Because if you try to help your partner by doing what you think he needs, he may feel better. Or he may not.

But if you help your partner by doing what your partner actually needs, then he will feel better. And act better.

And then you'll feel better too.

Read this when you each want different things

Whatever the issue – a major issue or a minor request – there'll always be times when you and your partner want different things. And there'll always be times when your different wants clash. When they do, it may seem as if the only alternatives are surrender or war.

There is another way, a way that's avoided conflict not only for couples, but also for countries.

Negotiation.

With negotiation, neither of you gives in or gives up. You don't hold your positions and stick to them for grim death. You don't act as if your own personal fulfilment is the only thing that matters.

Instead, you both agree to use all your skills to find as many solutions as possible. To be flexible enough to find solutions that work for both of you. To keep going until both of you are satisfied.

Because somewhere hidden away in almost every clash of wants is a solution that largely gives you both what you need.

Here's a way to do it, a negotiation process that works. There are eight steps. For each step, there are some sample questions you can use to move you on.

Don't worry if you take several hours, if not days, over it – though when you've learned how, you might get to a point where you can negotiate solutions in just a few minutes.

1: Say what you want

Then explore what lies behind what you want – your real needs: What do I really want ... What do you need here ... What's my real motivation?

2: Let go of all previous answers

Brainstorm from scratch, so creating more possibilities: What could we do? What else? No limits on money? No limits on energy?

3: Think of ways of getting more resources ...

... so creating yet more possibilities: Who could help? Where could we get ...? Who's got more information? What about finance?

4: Think through the pros and cons ...

... of each brainstormed option, even if you query it: What would be good about ...? What wouldn't work about ...? Why? Why not?

5: Think creatively round each option ...

... for ways to satisfy not just one but both: If we did this first, then that? Could we combine these two? How could we get to do both?

6: Set up safety nets

... so you don't feel locked in to one solution: What if that didn't work? How could we get out of it? How to prevent? Fallback plans?

7: Choose the most obvious option

If none spring up, either mark options out of ten and choose the highest, or go back to point 2 and brainstorm more options.

8: Plan how to put the option into practice

Agree a date to check progress – or renegotiate: Is it working? What could we do to make it better? What should we do instead?

If you find that for you, negotiation isn't working, here are four things to check:

- ♥ Are one or both of you being clear enough? If you don't know what you want, or don't tell your partner what you want, then the end result probably won't satisfy you.
- ♥ Are one or both of you being flexible enough? If you take up a position, defend it, stick rigidly to it and refuse to budge, then

you simply won't be able to move to a solution.

♥ Are one or both of you just too emotional to negotiate? This isn't a strategy to use if you're still feeling wobbly, blamey, aggressive or defensive. If you are, then get that sorted before you try to sort the issue. (See page 115 for a reminder of how to do this.)

♥ Are you settling for a solution that means just one of you is happy, not both? Negotiation only works, particularly over time, if both of you are satisfied with every decision. Otherwise, it's just oppression wrapped up to look good.

Read this if you're bored

Bored. Bored. Bored.

There's a point in most relationships when everything seems uninteresting. The sex, the conversation, the whole life you've built together – none of them get you going any more.

The most obvious reason for boredom is that there's not enough happening in your relationship. Since you've been together, you've had to pull back from interacting with the outside world. Maybe because of the kids, maybe because of the work, maybe because there's no money, you've limited your lives until there's nothing left to be interested in.

If that's the reason you're bored, then the answer is simple. Get a life.

- ♥ Cut back on the work, even just a bit.
- ♥ Get away from the kids, even just for an hour.
- ♥ Get more to be interested in – read more, watch more, do more.
- ♥ Make friends – other people can bring interest to your life.
- ♥ Make the TV your slave rather than vice versa.

When you start being more involved in the outside world, then your energy will climb. And you'll find that the world – and your relationship – isn't as boring as you thought.

Read this if you're seriously bored

Bored. Bored. Bored.

There's a point in most relationships when everything seems uninteresting. The sex, the conversation, the whole life you've built together – none of them get you going any more.

The hidden reason for boredom – the one no one talks about – is that there's too much happening in your relationship. Since you've been together, you've put each other through the mill. Maybe because of the rows, maybe because of the tears, maybe because of the insecurity, you got to a point where you felt too much about each other.

So eventually, you just shut down on the feelings. You anaesthetized yourselves against all emotions, until now you don't feel anything much about anything any more – including each other.

If that's the reason you're bored – or if nothing else has worked to sort the boredom – then the answer is complex. You need to face your feelings.

You need to realize and admit that there's resentment and anger and grief around. Then you need to find ways of sorting those emotions. Perhaps you can do that face to face, talking things through, forgiving and forgetting. More likely, you'll need the help of a counsellor to start really interacting with each other again.

But if you can start interacting, and if you do start interacting, then in the end the feelings will come back.

Simple truth about love

If the feeling's gone for you both, then don't assume
the love's gone too.

Feelings ebb and flow in a relationship.

And if you're in your relationship for the long haul,
you'll live through a lot of emotional tides.

Read this if you're growing apart

We were walking, as we often do, through country woods in Worcestershire. Summer woods, with sunlight filtering down through the leaves. Hillside woods, with trees as far as we could see above and below.

We came to a fork in the path. One fork seemed to go slightly up, the other slightly down. Nothing to choose between them, and they might diverge and completely separate us.

But the woods weren't that big – so one of us decided to take the up path, the other the down path. We set off, shouting occasionally to make sure we were still in touch.

And eventually, as we expected, the up path started to go down, the down path started to go up, both paths merged again – and we walked along together.

Sometimes, you and your partner seem to be on completely different paths. You've got different friends ... different hobbies ... different interests. These aren't just differences. These are the outward signs of two people living diverging lives.

You need to be careful. You need to take action so you don't drift too far apart.

So spend more time together. Do more talking together. Make a conscious effort to include each other, and get each other enthusiastic about your different passions. Remind each other, when you are together, that you still care. And keep the relationship central.

But if you do that, if you keep in emotional touch, then your paths will almost certainly merge again. It won't be a problem.

Read this if you're seriously growing apart

Sometimes, in your relationship, diverging paths will be a problem. Because sometimes not just your interests or hobbies, but your deepest needs are incompatible.

There are some needs which quite simply override any others – including love. These are the truly diverging paths that you may each take.

Fidelity

One of you needs fidelity. The other – whatever lip service they pay – doesn't want it ...

... Some rare couples make open relationships work. And many a partnership that's suffered an affair survives and triumphs. But if your partner consistently plays away when you don't want them to, or refuses to let you play away when you want to, then your relationship usually dies.

Having kids or not having kids

One of you is desperate to have children and the other is against it – or sufficiently unenthusiastic that they just keep postponing it ...

... Having a child – or living a childfree life – may mean more than anything to you. It may mean more to you than staying with your partner.

Sexual preference

What you like or don't like in bed doesn't fit. One of you gets turned-on by something that's neutral or a turn-off for the other ...

... If the problem is wanting sex versus not wanting it, then you may survive – particulary if the no-sex partner can turn a blind eye to affairs. But if each of you has a strong sexual need or preference that disgusts the other, the future's bleak.

Following a vision or vocation

One of you has always had a dream, and feels that if they don't fulfil that dream, then their whole life will be worthless ...

... When set against a lifetime fulfilment, a relationship may seem just too temporary and uninspiring.

These four key needs aren't ones that you naturally check out in the first rush of love or even the second rush of commitment. But they'll always lurk under the surface of the relationship like sharks under water. You may think your relationship's wonderful – it may actually be wonderful.

But sooner or later, you'll come back to talking about the issues that are more important than the relationship.

And then, you'll slowly realize you've made promises you can't keep.

Even if you've been together for ever and feel your partnership is as solid as a rock, if you feel strongly about any of the issues above but don't know what your partner currently feels, swap notes. Urgently.

Do it particularly if you started your relationship with one opinion – children would be off the agenda, for example – and have since switched opinions but haven't given your partner an update.

Of course, he may have changed his mind too and you may be back in sync again. But he may not have changed, he may still think as he did, and he may believe that you still think as you did. If so, you'll have to make some difficult choices.

The bottom line is that what's an essential need for one of you may be an optional extra for the other.

And if so, what's an essential relationship for one of you may become an optional extra for the other.

Read this if your commitment starts to feel wrong

The day after they started living together, Sarah's boyfriend mentioned in passing that their relationship wasn't for life.

At first, she thought she hadn't heard him correctly. They were both busy painting, each up a ladder at opposite ends of the hall. So she just laughed and called across 'For life, eh? That's a long time?'.

'No, ' he called back. 'I said *not* for life.'

There was a long silence. Sarah backed carefully down the ladder, turned round, sat on the bottom step and said 'Excuse me?'

At the very point where she had started to relax, secure that they'd made a commitment, he'd started to tense up and look for escape routes.

Because when we make a commitment ... when we move from being partners to living together ... from living together to being engaged ... from being engaged to being husband and wife ... (or from being husband and wife to being parents) ... along with the feeling of commitment may also come a sensation of pure panic.

Yes, it's good knowing that we're big enough and grown up enough to make a serious commitment. But with those goodies come responsibilities. We can start to feel trapped by everything we have to do, both now, and in the future relationship. 'Till death do us part' feels like a life sentence.

And as with all big moves in life, when we make a commitment, our relationship can take on whole layers of new expectation. Now we're committed, we may think we have to earn more ... stay at home more ... have sex less ... behave like husband and wife, whatever that means. And we may not want to play Mummies and Daddies. Or we may want to, but our partner doesn't.

We may never adapt. Many a new spouse has made a bid for freedom as the plane touched down after the honeymoon. Or has tried to live the single life – hanging out with friends all the time, staying at work until all hours, spending money as if there's no tomorrow. And as if there'd been no vows.

The key to avoiding commitment-panic is to get clear just what you're buying into. Nowadays, you can be a good wife and not wear a pinny, be a great husband and not wash the car at weekends. As long as you both agree the ground rules, and have the courage to carry them out, commitment can be what you make it.

So whenever you go through a major commitment shift, check out the basics to make sure you expect the same deal. If you don't expect the same, talk things through and keep talking them through until you get understanding and agreement.

Here are 12 things to check out with each other as you move into a new relationship commitment:

♥ Who now does the housework, cooking, shopping?
♥ Who now has to work and who doesn't?
♥ Whose work is most important?
♥ Who makes the money decisions?
♥ Who makes 'where do we live?' decisions?
♥ Has our commitment to our families changed?
♥ Is it still OK to have separate friends?
♥ How much time should we now spend together?

♥ Will our sex life change, and if so how?

♥ What secrets should always be shared?

♥ What's the aim of this commitment (stability, companionship, having children ...)?

♥ Are we heading for futher commitment, or is this it?

Two final hints. First, get the power stuff sorted. A lot of commitment panic – for women as well as men – is because people feel they've signed their autonomy away along with the mortgage or the marriage certificate. So make sure that equality in the relationship isn't just there but is also seen to be there. Look back at the 'control' sections of this book, on pages 79 to 94, and take on board what you read there.

Second, keep reminding yourself, and your partner, of the goodies that come with your new commitment. The grass can seem more yellow and barren once you're on this side of the hill. And the security, protection, acceptance and love that were the motivation for your commitment may be forgotten once they're part of your daily reality. So think and talk, regularly about what you're getting now that you weren't getting before. And as you do, count your blessings.

Sarah and her boyfriend? Well, what followed his passing comment was the worst row they'd ever had. But they kept talking, and kept working at it. They're still together ten-and-a-half-years later. Happy, married and with two toddlers.

Simple truth about love

When you first made a commitment to each other, it seemed like you were the only two people in the world.

Wrong.

There's a world full of exciting people out there. And some of them will come up to the door of your relationship, and ask to be let in.

You need to know what you're going to do when the bell rings.

Read this if you're jealous

The following disaster happened to a friend of mine, though I was actually there when it all went pearshaped.

She'd noticed for a few weeks that her husband was being secretive, that he put the phone down when she came into the room, whisked letters into his briefcase bag when she passed behind him.

And though he had never in their long marriage looked at another woman, she began to wonder. She was particularly aware that the years were ticking away – the words 'trading in' and 'new model' came inexorably to mind.

She asked him jokingly if he was having an affair and he laughed. She asked him seriously if he was having an affair and he got irritated. She rang him at work to suggest a romantic meal to make up, and his secretary went all coy and said he'd had to leave the office unexpectedly. She began to panic – and it was probably that panic that was responsible for what happened next.

One Friday, she'd arranged to go out briefly with a friend. They drove round to their local pub, sat in the window seat and chatted. And it was at that point that she looked out and saw her husband driving past, with a woman's figure half seen, in the passenger seat. She froze.

Then she went into attack mode. Ignoring her friend's protestations, she sprang to her feet, half-walked and half-ran to the car park, and drove like a madwoman. She followed her husband's headlights as he drove on for about half a mile, and then turned off. To their house.

My friend slowed her car into the driveway, only half registering that her friend had followed from the pub. She leapt out, slammed the car door and had her key in the lock instantly. As she burst through, her words 'How dare you bring your lover into our house!' rang out clearly.

Clearly to everyone there, all busily putting up the decorations for her surprise birthday party. To all her friends – bar the one who'd lured her out to the pub. To all her colleagues from work – including her boss. And to her sister – whom her husband had just picked up from the station.

And every single one of them had just heard her accuse him of adultery ...

This story may make you cringe, but it's not surprising. When a partner seems to love someone else, then most of us would panic. And if a partner does love someone else, then panicking is absolutely appropriate.

But sometimes what we're seeing isn't what is happening at all. And we still panic.

We still jump immediately to the worst conclusion. Then we feel bad about that conclusion, think it means we're second best, or that our partner is a swine, and that everything is falling apart. Then, we throw a wobbly. When all along, there's been absolutely nothing to worry about.

If your partner has a track record of playing away, then this section doesn't apply to you – instead, you need to be on your guard, if not on your way! But if you recognize yourself in my friend's story – or if other people have told you that you run jealousy patterns – then be brave and start doing things differently.

Learn to see what is really happening rather than what you're afraid is happening

Look clearly at what your partner's doing rather than rushing to think the worst. If you find it hard to make objective judgements, get a trusted friend (not your partner) to tell you what they think is true and what they think you're hallucinating.

Learn to remember track record

If over the years your partner has never shown the slightest interest in betraying you, has been content with you and proud of your relationship, keep that clearly and firmly in mind when you're tempted to wobble.

Learn not to do things that will harm

It's tempting to keep on at your partner, questioning, asking for reassurance, insisting he accounts for every second of his time. But how would you react if your partner did this to you? Quite right, you'd hate it. And if it carried on, you'd leave. So will he, eventually.

Learn to do things that will help

Sometimes, you need to back off and simply trust. Not every partner who's trusted stays faithful. But a partner who isn't trusted rarely stays.

Learn to separate what is happening from what you feel about yourself

The worse you feel about yourself, the worse you'll feel about your partner paying even the slightest amount of harmless social attention to anyone else. So do whatever you can to boost your confidence and self-esteem.

If you believe that you're worth loving, then your partner's much more likely to believe it too.

Read this if he's jealous

Living with a jealous partner can feel like living in a cage. You love him to bits, but he's so insecure. He worries about where you go, what you do, most of all who you're with. You know it's because he loves you, but you still feel trapped.

Here are six guidelines to remember and act on:

♥ Just because he's jealous doesn't mean to say that you shouldn't be loyal. Be squeaky clean in your dealings with him, always honest, always faithful.

♥ Just because he's jealous doesn't mean to say that you can't have a life. Insist on your right to have personal freedom, without restriction or pressure.

♥ Just because he's jealous doesn't mean to say that you can't challenge him. Help your partner think through his fears and see how irrational they are.

♥ Just because he's jealous doesn't mean to say that you shouldn't support him. Help him build his self-esteem so he starts to believe he's worthy of your love.

♥ Just because he's jealous doesn't mean to say he can't recover. Encourage him to go to counselling to help him overcome his problem.

♥ Just because he's jealous doesn't mean to say you've got to stay. If your partner's jealousy is greater than his love, then seriously consider making your escape.

Read this if you lust after someone else

One of the things no one tells you when you fall desperately in lust with your partner is this:

At some time in the future, you'll almost certainly fall desperately in lust with someone else.

Because it's a total myth that commitment means that your hormones get blinkered and never look elsewhere. Even in the best relationships, you'll fancy other people physically and emotionally, and they'll fancy you. And if they tell you they fancy you – by saying it straight, or just by the way they look at you – then you'll fancy them even more.

Hormones don't wear wedding rings. And hormones are ever so susceptible to flattery.

If this happens to you, there's no need to criticize yourself. Lust is almost inevitable, and it doesn't mean you've stopped loving your partner.

Equally, there's really no need to criticize your relationship. Lusting doesn't mean you're with the wrong person, and that you should go off and start again with someone new. That option may be very tempting, particularly as established love is always harder work than brand-shining-new love. But attraction to someone else, mentally or physically, is a natural event. Not a foolproof signal that you need to trade in what you've currently got.

But you do need to think carefully about your next move. Because there's a big difference between what you feel and what you do.

And there's all the difference in the world between wanting to go to bed with someone and actually doing it.

Yes, having an affair may make you feel good about yourself. It may add excitement to your life. It may make you feel important again, when in your relationship you haven't felt important for a long time. And, of course, it may actually be what you need to lever yourself out of a partnership that is now completely wrong for you.

But having an affair also changes your relationship. For ever. And often for the worst.

So, enjoy your lust when it happens. It almost certainly will. But think carefully about putting that enjoyment into action.

Think particularly about these crucial questions:

♥ Do I know what having an affair will do to my partner? Do I care?

♥ Do I know what having an affair will do to my lover (or my lover's partner)? Do I care?

♥ What do I feel if I imagine the moment when my partner finds out that I've had an affair?

♥ Did the lust I feel for my partner fade? Will the lust I feel for my lover also fade?

♥ If I look back in five years, what do I think will have happened if I have an affair?

♥ And what does all this tell me about my relationship with my existing partner ... with my potential lover ... and about what I should do now?

Read this if you suspect he lusts after someone else

The suspicion gradually dawns on you, and it's horrifying. Your partner has started to fancy someone other than you.

Lusting after other people is natural – and you won't stop him doing it. But will he put that lust into practice, and so rock the boat? It's best to do a risk assessment.

Here are six risk factors that make it more likely your partner may be playing away, or thinking seriously about playing away:

♥ He's been unfaithful to you before.
♥ He's been unfaithful to anyone before, even if you were the person he was unfaithful with.
♥ He's recently had a setback that has made him need an ego boost.
♥ He's recently had a key birthday that has made him panic about his age.
♥ Your relationship is going through a tricky patch.
♥ You've stopped having sex with each other.

If you guess, reading that list, that there's a high risk of putting lust into action, then you need to act. Is there anything you can do? Yes, lots.

Do get appropriate support for yourself

When you suspect an affair, you can feel not only betrayed but also isolated. The person you've trusted all these years, the person you normally talk problems through with, has now put themselves on the side of the enemy. So do get yourself support – someone you can talk to, who will accept your emotions and help you think through what to do now.

But choose carefully – spilling the beans to a best friend may mean that they take against your partner for ever, even if your suspicions prove unjustified or if you eventually reconcile again. It might be better to trust your unclear situation to a professional friend – a counsellor – at least to begin with.

Do get closer to her

If you know the person he's probably lusting after, one good move is to get close to her (or, conceivably, him). This will subtly disturb whatever is going on, and may make one or both of them pull back. But it won't completely stop what's happening. And it won't solve the problem the next time he lusts after someone else.

Do take notice if what you feel is relief

Relief at a partner's affair – actual or potential – is a sign that your commitment is slipping and more than likely, you want out. Have a 'where are we at' talk and then either work on improving your relationship. Or part.

Do choose carefully whether to front him or not

If your partner isn't having an affair, then talking through your concerns will almost always help – unless you run a jealousy number in which case see page 133 for better ways to handle the situation.

If he is having an affair, then fronting him up about it may precipitate a crisis. He may feel he has to choose between you and her – and he may not choose you. Personally I would always challenge an unfaithful partner. But you may prefer the safer option of lying low and letting things blow over.

If the worst comes to the worst, do be clear about what you want

Much of the real heartache after an affair's discovered is because one or both of you simply doesn't know whether you want to split up or carry on. So take the initiative. Spend time thinking. Talk it through with (trustworthy) friends. See a counsellor if you want to.

Decide what you want and tell your partner, rather than letting him dictate terms – and then realizing later that you didn't like the terms he dictated.

Whatever you decide, remember this. Many couples who face infidelity and use it as a motivation to improve their relationship succeed; they often say their partnership is stronger than before. On the other hand, most women who leave unfaithful partners say that they should have done it years ago.

So actually, so long as you do what feels right to you, in the end you are almost certain to win.

Simple truth about love

♥ There's no such thing as a relationship without differences.

♥ And so mostly, there's no such thing as a relationship without disagreements.

♥ And so mostly, there's no such thing as a relationship without conflicts.

♥ It's lucky then that mostly, there's no such thing as a conflict that a good relationship can't resolve.

Read this if you're having a bad time emotionally

I'm a great fan of emotion.

I like being scared. I'm terrified of heights – so naturally I've spent a good few holidays walking on precipitous clifftops with a thousand-foot drop to the sea below.

I love a good cry. My idea of the perfect 'home alone' is a large box of paper hankies and *Truly, Madly, Deeply* on the video.

I even adore a good rant, and have been known in my time to throw spaghetti – cooked and uncooked – in the heat of the moment. Well, the kitchen ceiling needed painting anyway.

But when it comes to running a relationship, I'm also wary of emotion.

I think it's had far too good a press.

Because the way we tend to see love nowadays is as a completely emotional event. We begin by being overwhelmed by attraction and overcome by lust. Then we're euphoric as that attraction and lust are returned. As time goes by, we feel anxious – when things don't go too well. Or angry – when we don't get what we want.

And if our emotion seems to be dying, then we presume that love is dying too. And that there's nothing else to do apart from leave.

Yet emotions are only a part of love. And often they're the most unreliable part. Because emotions were developed by nature as hair trigger signals to tell us when something's important or dangerous, to get us up and doing, fleeing for our lives or turning to fight. They hit our nervous system at a run, pumping adrenaline and boosting our heart rate. That can feel wonderful. But it isn't necessarily the best basis on which to create a partnership that's going to last.

Because emotions are there to tell you what to do short-term. And that might not be what's best to do in a long-term relationship.

Emotions urge you on to act immediately and precipitous-ly. And that might not be what's best to do when you want to develop a lasting commitment.

Emotions tell you what to do to save yourself. And that might not be what's best to do when there's two of you to consider.

So by all means feel as much as you can in your relation-ship. Experience your emotions, don't push them down. Particularly, feel the good feelings – the euphoria, the ecstasy, the lust. And don't ignore the more painful feelings – guilt, irritation, worry – because they're useful signs that some-thing needs to change.

But don't necessarily act on those painful feelings. When things are going wrong between you and your partner, have the courage to stop and think. Do your best to understand why what is happening is happening – why you're getting stuck. Find out what will work and then do it, rather than let-ting your emotions drive you into the first possible response and then regretting it.

And don't think it's cheating to use practical down-to-earth solutions to solve emotional problems. If you feel bad, the answer may not be to concentrate on changing the feel-ings – trying desperately to cheer up or calm down. The answer may be to steadily and deliberately change things – by

talking, by arrangement, by negotiation – so that you naturally feel better.

If there's one key to making your relationship work it's
contained in six words. Words which sound unromantic.
Sound too pragmatic. Sound horribly sensible. Words which
are these ...

If loving doesn't work, try thinking.

Read this if bad days keep turning into nightmare evenings

There's an Alan Parker film called *Bugsy Malone* that's a long-time favourite of mine. It's the story of Al Capone – but acted by children, who take the age-old themes of love and hate and death and somehow replay them in a way that's both incredibly meaningful and enchantingly violence-free.

In that film, instead of deadly submachine guns, the kids have splurge guns, that shoot out cream not bullets. And at the end of the film, all the 'splurged' characters miraculously reappear on screen to show that the gunfire wasn't serious.

Some of the time, if you and your partner fire harsh words at each other, it's serious. But a lot of the time, particularly if you're living together and so automatically bring the world back home with you each evening, one partner's being sharp or ratty with the other isn't serious – or even particularly personal.

So if your bad times typically happen at the end of the day, when you're tired, edgy, ground down, frustrated by other things and other people, then you don't need to panic.

What you do need is to see things differently. If you can see each other's irritation as simply splurging, a cream-filled volley with no malice intended, then it magically becomes harmless. You can step back, watch each other fire, and emerge totally unscathed. It won't destroy your relationship.

In fact, supporting each other to let go of all the frustrations of the day will positively build your love, because it will build the sense that you're accepted even if you're not perfect with each other.

The next time either of you is in a bad mood because of outside pressures, actively make time and space for that bad mood. Agree that whichever of you is under pressure is allowed to splurge.

Here are the rules of good splurging:

♥ Set a time limit – say ten minutes.

♥ Agree a cut-off time – say, until the children come home.

♥ Get out the paper hankies.

♥ Bar insults, alcohol and violence.

♥ Otherwise, all whinges, rants, tears, complaints are OK.

♥ Other partner to give attention and acceptance.

♥ Take turns, if you both need splurge time.

When time's up, then all bets are off. All evil behaviour stops for the day, all frustrations and resentments get put back in their box and forgotten. Splurge guns are unloaded.

But just firing them, in a wonderful burst of pent-up emotion, will have helped.

Just saying what has made you feel bad will have made you feel good again.

Read this if you fight

You've been there. Of course you have.

One minute there's nothing wrong and you're laughing at his jokes. The next minute, one of you gets irritable. You raise an eyebrow. He makes a sharp comment. You snap. He shouts. Two minutes later you're both checking the number of the divorce lawyer in the phone book.

You've just encountered the 'Zillmann Transfer of Excitation Effect'. Dolf Zillman, a psychologist at the University of Alabama, researched emotion – specifically anger. And what he found was that if one person feels anger, then that anger (or excitation) will transfer itself over to another person – whether or not the original bad feeling was aimed at them.

This emotional infection makes sense. In early human groups, before we had words, it was useful to pick up feelings from each other so we acted together to defend, attack, run away.

But picking up feelings in this way from each other is a problem where love is concerned.

Because if you feel irritated or frustrated or angry – even if that's with the world in general and not with each other – then you'll often find yourselves in trouble. In the same way as a flame leaps across from one burning house to another, or one burning field to another, you'll trigger each other all the way into a blazing row.

When you fight, this is what happens, step by tiny step:

1 You notice your partner's angry body language.
2 So you start to think negatively about him.

3 So your body floods with adrenaline because you're angry.

4 So your body language tenses.

So, within seconds:

5 Your partner notices your angry body language.

6 So he starts to think negatively about you.

7 So his body floods with adrenaline because he's angry.

8 So his body language tenses.

And so on.

But you can stop all this. If you or your partner seem to be getting angry, then you can stop the rage leaping from one to the other of you. All you have to do is to take any step of the process and halt it. All you have to do is create a fire break.

1: Instead of noticing your partner's angry body language ...

... try becoming aware of the nervous tension that he's showing. Anger is a reaction to being threatened – it is, in fact, the other side of fear. Anyone who's angry is also afraid. If you see your partner get angry, notice also that he's anxious and scared. Respond to his fear, not his anger, and you'll find yourself feeling compassion not rage.

2: Instead of starting to think negative thoughts about your partner ...

... challenge the negativity. If you can think positively about your partner, you will cool things out. So remember that your partner normally behaves well towards you. Find mitigating circumstances – he's tired or stressed. Remember the good times – you've been so happy lately. Put things in perspective – it's only a little row.

3: Instead of flooding your body with adrenaline ...

... work off the adrenaline by deliberately relaxing – deep breathing is the easiest way.

4: Instead of tensing your body language ...

... deliberately alter your body language to look more relaxed and friendly. Stand more easily. Uncross your arms. Lean forward. If you can, smile – which even if it's a little forced will de-tense your whole body and signal to your partner that you're at least trying to be relaxed and sympathetic.

You can also create a fire break by stepping in to interrupt your partner's reactions – by shifting what he thinks, what he feels and what he does.

5: Instead of your partner's noticing your angry body language ...

... make him aware of what else you feel underneath the anger. Explain 'I've really had a bad day – that's all ... I'm annoyed with the kids, not with you ... I'm so scared we're going to have another row.' Let him see your vulnerability and he'll immediately feel more like supporting you.

love coach

6: Instead of allowing your partner to think negative thoughts about you ...

... step in to replace the positive thoughts with negative ones. Remind him of your commitment – 'I do want us to work this out ...'. Tell him you understand – ' I'm sorry you're feeling like this ...'. Encourage him to think about the future – ' I know we can get through it'.

7: Instead of allowing your partner to flood with adrenaline ...

... let him take time alone. One of the best ways to stop feeling angry, particularly for men, is to be on their own for a while. About twenty minutes 'time out' will usually do the trick, particularly if he can do something – like reading or watching television – that stops him brooding.

8: Instead of letting your partner's body language tense even more ...

... help him to relax by offering contact. Men often get overwhelmed with words, particularly when those words are hostile. But men relax when they're offered touch.

So look into his eyes. Smile at him. Hold hands. Give him a hug.

Make your peace.

Read this if you keep on fighting

Money, housework, children, sex ... these are the core things people fight over. Aren't they?

Actually, no. Those are the surface things that people fight over. Underneath that surface, there are deeper issues – and as long as you don't resolve them, you'll just carry on fighting.

So if you and your partner argue regularly or constantly – about anything and everything, about nothing at all – then you may actually be arguing about these deeper-level things.

♥ You both fight for safety. The deeper issue is about being let down, betrayed or abandoned by your partner. You defend to protect yourself.

♥ You both fight for respect. The deeper issue is about feeling your partner doesn't consider or appreciate you. You attack to prove you're worthwhile.

♥ You both fight for autonomy. The deeper issue is about who has the control in the relationship. You argue to make sure you at least have equal say in what's happening.

There is, of course, a problem. There are two of you doing all this. Two of you defending, attacking, arguing.

So it's a vicious circle. Faced with the other's bad behaviour, either one of you is going to fight back – for safety, for respect, for control. And then the other one fights back harder, for their own safety, respect and control.

If you recognize your arguments in these descriptions,

then you've taken a vital step forward. Because once you know what underpins your rows, there's a lot you can do to reduce the general conflict level in your relationship. The secret is simple – on a day to day basis, make sure that you're each getting what you need, by making your relationship a safe place, a respectful place, a place where both of you feel you have an equal say in things.

Plus, once you know what underpins your rows, there's a lot you can do to stop any single row in its tracks. Literally, you can break the vicious circle.

Though it does take nerve. You have to step outside the combat zone. And you have to offer your partner something which may feel difficult, scary, even pointless.

You have to give your partner what he needs.

Offering safety

If you sense that your partner feels insecure, and is arguing in order to protect himself ...

... you can break the vicious circle by allowing your partner to feel safer. This doesn't mean being vulnerable yourself. It does mean doing whatever you can to lower the aggression level.

Bite back threatening words. Quieten your voice and slow things down. Offer to touch your partner if you know he'll respond to that – not if he'll feel trapped by it. Whatever his deepest fear is – that you'll leave, that you're pressuring him, that you don't understand him – say what you genuinely can to show him those fears are groundless.

Offering respect

If you sense that your partner feels unappreciated, and is arguing in order to prove himself ...

... you can break the vicious circle by allowing your partner to feel more respected. This doesn't mean saying that you're not OK. It does mean doing whatever you can to show him that he's OK.

Bite back insulting or mocking words. Speak warmly and affectionately. You don't need to agree with your partner, but you do need to acknowledge what he's saying – and let him know that you do. It will also work to tell him what he's doing well – in general, in your relationship, and even during the current argument!

Offering autonomy

If you sense that your partner feels controlled, and is arguing in order to have an equal say ...

... you can break the vicious circle by allowing your partner to feel freer and more autonomous. This doesn't mean giving in. It does mean doing whatever you can to avoid powerplays.

Bite back controlling words and avoid 'trapping' your partner with logical argument – or any physical manoeuvres such as blocking his way. Ask what he wants, listen to it, acknowledge it. Then make it clear you're committed to spending time and energy until he, as well as you, gets his needs met.

Remember that none of the above means that you have to give in, or give up. We're not talking about submitting to

your partner, compromising – or even agreeing.

We're talking about using words and body language to reduce his insecurity, reassure him he's respected, let him know he's not being controlled. After you've done that, and he starts to feel better, you can both start getting things sorted to your mutual satisfaction.

These strategies aren't surrender. They're battle management. They go straight to the heart of what creates arguments. Yes, after you've both calmed down, you may have to sort the disagreement that sparked the row in the first place. And when sorting it, you have to keep going until you're both happy with the outcome.

But if even one of you is reassured that you're safe, respected and in equal charge, then sorting things will be a thousand per cent easier.

And as always, these strategies also start creating a different climate within your relationship. Because when you react in these positive ways, you actually teach your partner a new way of behaving – to offer you the safety, respect and control you need, and so take away any reasons you may have to keep fighting.

It may take a while, but once he learns how, your partner can be a peacemaker too.

Read this if you can't seem to kiss and make up

Coming back together after a row can be a bit like walking up a bank of shingle. One slip and you slide.

Because most times after a row, you're both still edgy. You want to kiss and make up, but you're also wary of being attacked again. Or having to defend again. One sharp comment ... one flinch ... and you're sliding back to the bottom of the same stuff, feeling bad and lashing out.

Here are three things to remember when you're trying to get back together and can't:

♥ How you feel will be how your partner feels. If you're still angry, he will be too. If you can somehow be calm – not submissive, but positively steady and loving – it's more likely that's what you'll get back.

♥ Apologizing isn't a surrender – it just means you regret what happened, and hope it won't happen again. Love isn't 'never having to say you're sorry'. It's being willing to say you're sorry because that helps you both contact your love again.

♥ If you don't sort the issues, then the row will happen again until you do. So unless your argument has been entirely due to stress and strain and isn't about anything concrete, always sit down and talk through the disagreement. And get it sorted.

Remember there's no point in hanging on to the bad feeling. If you keep reminding yourself, or your partner, of how painful it felt to row, you'll find yourself feeling so bad that you row again. After you've made up your differences, let the anger go.

Simple truth about love

If you think that some relationships don't have bad times, then you're wrong.

Good relationships have bad times and weather them, survive them.

The best relationships have bad times and learn from them, triumph through them.

While bad relationships have bad times and cling on to them for grim death.

And so, in the end, get destroyed by them.

Read this if the past still hurts

On the morning after her wedding night, in a steady and relentless downpour of rain, Catherine murdered her marriage.

That was sixty years ago.

Catherine and Harry had courted for a year, and grown more and more sure of their feelings. In Catherine's case, sure particularly that here was a man who was kind, patient, and would never ever explode in fury in the way her father did regularly and for no real reason.

So when Harry asked her to marry him, Catherine said an unhesitating 'yes'. She went up the aisle with her eyes wide open, and her faith intact. And the morning after their wedding night, in a glow of romance, they got up early, walked out arm-in-arm from their honeymoon hotel to the promenade, looked out over the sea – and the heavens opened.

As they rushed for shelter, Harry let fly. It was raining, and he didn't want it to be raining, and he didn't want everything to be spoiled when it was all so wonderful.

Catherine stood and listened to him rant, and she grew quieter and quieter and more and more appalled. It was the first time he'd ever been less than calm in her presence. She realized that she was married – irrevocably, according to the rules of sixty years ago – to a man who got angry.

There's no blame here. Harry wasn't a violent man; he just felt annoyed and showed it – and the only shame was that he'd been so scared of losing Catherine that he'd never dared show her any negative feelings before.

Catherine wasn't to blame; but she was already vulnerable from her father's rages, and she'd never learned to shrug off other people's bad temper as being just what they were ... temporary bad emotions.

There's no blame. But there is a tragedy. Because they did kiss and make up, but Catherine didn't forgive and forget. And she never did forget, as the days, the weeks and the months went by and Harry proved to be a loving – and generally good tempered – husband.

Catherine never trusted him again. She never trusted their relationship again. And she spent the next sixty years being wary ...

If there's some past event – big or small – in your relationship that still keeps hurting you, please sort it. One way or the other.

If what's happened is a betrayal that you just can't live with and you never will, admit that. Don't waste a single minute more stumbling on in resentment and bitterness and trying to make things work. Have the courage and compassion – for your partner if not for yourself – to let go of the relationship.

But if you possibly can, let go of the resentment instead. Yes, that feels dangerous. We think that if we forgive and forget what happened, then it'll happen again. Resentment is our mind's way of trying to protect ourselves from future pain – by reminding us of past pain, and then keeping us on full alert against the same thing ever happening again.

It's a bad strategy. Resentment seems to protect us but in fact just keeps us feeling rotten. We can never really enjoy our relationship here and now. And our partner always lives under a cloud – whether he knows it or not.

There are ways of forgiving. People do it all the time, and are glad they did. And if you can contact your strength and your love, one of these ways may work for you.

Here are five things that may have happened. If you can now realize that they have happened, it may now mean you can forgive and forget.

♥ The painful event has disappeared over time. It's faded into insignificance because your partner and your relationship have been wonderful since then.

♥ The painful event seems irrelevant, unimportant or harmless. It hasn't badly affected you, so there's nothing to forgive

♥ The painful event has been regretted. Your partner has now realized how badly he's hurt you, and you're sure he'd never hurt you like that again.

♥ The painful event has been explained. You understand why your partner did what he did, you sympathize with it, and you realize he did the best he could in the circumstances.

♥ The painful event was partly down to you. You now realize that you share responsibility because of something you did or said that created the situation.

Think about these possibilities. See if, over time, you could take any of them on board. The hard fact is that if you don't then, like Catherine, in sixty years time, you'll have held on to your memories.

But in the meantime, you'll have completely let go of your love. And wasted your life.

Read this if you want to kill him

When Lucy found herself gazing irritably at her partner as he sat at the kitchen table – and then looking purposefully down at the bread knife in her hand – she realized that what she was feeling was not exactly love.

It was at that point that she put the knife firmly down on the bread board, marched over to Paul and said 'we have to talk'.

It wasn't that he'd done anything to annoy her. That was the point. There'd been no blazing row, no deep disagreement. But over the past few days, Lucy had found herself simply getting more and more irritated with him. And that irritation had suddenly flared, tipped over in a way she didn't quite understand.

It took a while to understand it – and the exact explanation was never really clear. It had something to do with Paul working long hours, being under stress, and cutting off from Lucy. Plus a far-off memory of her father getting sick and cutting off in the same way, and of eight-year-old Lucy trying to reach him, trying and trying and trying – and meeting only the gentle and weary disengagement of the terminally ill.

A combination of unresolved grief and pure fury at her father for dying had stirred up things in Lucy that had just overwhelmed her.

Because sometimes, however much you love your partner, you feel a sudden rush of totally irrational rage towards him. And even if you don't find yourself fingering a bread knife, you certainly want to slap him, very hard.

We're not talking about irritation, but about a feeling so strong it can seem as if it's taking over your whole body. And we're not talking about an appropriate response to your partner being violent or abusive. We're talking about you hating him when he's done nothing serious to you – when what he's done is something that normally you wouldn't have noticed it at all.

Almost always, these waves of fury aren't anything to do with what's happening in real life. They don't mean that there's something wrong with your relationship. Or with you or with your partner. All they mean is that something has pushed your buttons. And that the buttons that were pushed are very deep, very painful, and probably very old.

As with Lucy, there was someone in your past who hurt you. They may not have meant to, but they rejected you most likely, or ignored you, or scared you. Maybe when you were a child, maybe in your early relationships, certainly in a way that you couldn't do anything about back then, or couldn't resolve in your mind and heart.

And now, when your partner nudges that memory, the feelings come flooding back. You almost certainly won't remember where they came from. But they're here.

If you feel this sort of fury towards your partner, don't fall for it. It's not real, it's not really anything to do with what's happening here and now.

Hold back on the action. Of course you're tempted to pull the plug out of his freshly-run bath – just before he steps into it. Of course you're tempted to cut the seat out of his best trousers – with him in them. Or hurt him. Or hurt yourself. Don't do it.

Instead, put your energy into calming down. Breathe deeply, relax as much as you can, get out if you feel you might lash out.

Once the crisis is over, put some time and energy into thinking through exactly what memories have been stirred, who the real villain of the piece was, back in your past. And if you remember, then by all means imagine slicing them to pieces slowly.

Yes, if your anger highlights something you need to change in your relationship, then change it. But this kind of fury usually doesn't; it's a ghost from the past. So don't let it come back to haunt your here and now relationship.

So as far as your partner is concerned, let the fury die. Be kind – even extra kind for a while, if you want to offset the natural nastiness that's spinning off towards them in the wake of your bad moods.

Here are three things to tell yourself if you feel you want to slap (or kill) your partner:

♥ This isn't about what's happening now. This is about what happened then.

♥ I don't need to act on this, I just need to feel it.

♥ Just because I hate my partner doesn't mean I don't love him.

Read this if other people mess up your relationship

The most public row I ever witnessed nearly ended in tragedy. And I – along with the other 50 people there – was largely to blame.

I was in one of those pubs in London which is half in the open air and half under cover, and where what you're saying is typically drowned out by the street performers.

Which is probably why, when one of the couples on the next table started arguing, and when their argument flared into a full scale battle, the other customers had no qualms at all about being spectators.

I've no idea what the row was about. Neither did anyone else watching. But when she stood up and called him a bastard, there was a chorus of voices telling him what to do next. And when what he did next was to pour a pint of beer over her, suddenly it became a circus. Through sheer nervous excitement we all stood round and cheered her on.

She smashed the glass on the table and stood there holding the jagged edge.

Most of us fell silent immediately, though one or two kept shouting. But thank God they were hushed by the crowd, and then one of her friends said something to her quietly, and someone else took the glass from her hand. And she was hurried off to the ladies, and he and his mate sat there ashen-faced.

I was left, sobered both literally and emotionally, wondering whether – if we hadn't stopped when we did – something very nasty indeed might have happened.

If it had, I think we bystanders would have been just as responsible as she was.

Because though love feels like something private and hidden, never influenced by what others say and do, in fact bystanders of all kinds have a direct effect on what happens.

So other people may trigger problems just by their existence. Without saying a word they make it clear that they don't approve of your partner, or of your partnership. Then you're left questioning your love – or struggling to keep loyal to your partner without betraying your parents, your sister, your best friend or your boss.

Other people may trigger problems by active interference. They'll tell you what they'd do in your situation – even though they don't know anything about your situation. Or they'll show you what they wished they'd done when they were in your situation – giving you their advice to themselves, with hindsight and many years out of date.

And other people may, just occasionally, trigger problems out of sheer maliciousness. You're doing well and they're not. Or you're doing badly and they're glad of it. So they push you firmly towards the edge of disaster, and laugh as they see you topple.

This doesn't mean to say that you should never ever lean on anyone for support in your relationship. Friends, family, community or religious elders, professional counsellors – all these people can and do offer you invaluable support.

What it does mean is that if you feel that people around you are affecting your relationship badly, then you are probably right. And that you need to follow a few basic rules to keep your relationship safe from the crowd:

Think before whingeing

Constantly offloading your resentments about your partner will undermine the relationship. People will almost always agree with you – they'll get caught up in your emotion. And their agreement will make you feel even worse about your relationship, so even less able to put positive energy into sorting it.

Don't enrol others

Asking people to take sides is unfair on them. And it's unwise for you. It may feel good to have someone agreeing with your point of view against your partner. But it's impossible to bring a fight to a cooperative conclusion while supporters are cheering for blood.

Steer clear of relationship mud; it sticks

If you're feeling vulnerable, don't spend all your time swapping notes with other people who're also going through problems. It may feel like a meeting of minds, but you may catch their unhappiness by osmosis – and add their relationship-spoiler strategies to your own.

Take early love with a pinch of salt

Don't be wobbled by seeing a blissful new relationship. Early ecstasy rarely lasts. The couple who spent all New Year's Eve feeding each other strawberries will be the ones who at the next Christmas party are hissing in the kitchen.

Learn from proven relationship heaven

But if you know a long-lasting couple who still seem deeply in love, ask them to be your mentors. They obviously know something you don't.

And if you ask them nicely, they'll tell you what it is.

Read this if things are just too hard

Love conquers all. Not.

There are some things that can't be sorted just by loving alone.

You may have done everything you possibly can to feel right and to act right, and to get your partner to act right. But things still aren't working.

And by that time, things are also confused. Particularly if there's conflict, you may be stuck in thinking that all the problems are your fault and so all that's needed is for you to pull yourself together.

Or if your partner alternates between behaving badly and behaving well, you may have got stuck in enduring the bad times and hanging on hopefully for the good times.

You may not have realized that things are seriously bad, that it's time to get help, or get out. You may not know when to say 'enough'.

Here are 10 clear signals that you need to say 'enough' in your relationship:

- ♥ Your work is suffering because of your relationship problems.
- ♥ Your relationship with your children is suffering.
- ♥ You're feeling out of control about what's happening.
- ♥ You go to bed every night unhappy.
- ♥ Both of you believe that only one of you is to blame for what's happening.
- ♥ You have aggressive arguments more days than not.

♥ One or both of you is getting physically ill as a result of the strain of the relationship.

♥ One or both of you is getting depressed or suffering other emotional illness.

♥ The relationship has started to include drinking, drug-taking, compulsive gambling, or violence.

♥ You can't talk about your pain with your partner. Because if you start, he says that there simply isn't a problem.

If you spot any of these signals in your partnership, then turn to page 235 and use the resources you find there to take action, get extra support, or call in the experts.

Simple truth about love

Not all relationships are destroyed from within, because you feel bad, or argue, or fight to the death.

Many relationships are destroyed from the outside, by constant pressures, by once-in-a-lifetime crises.

So if you're being attacked by the world ...

... first protect each other.

Read this if you don't spend enough time together

One of the nicest colleagues I have works hard. But he always finds time for fun, for games, for other people. He has a notice on his office desk, and I see it whenever we have a meeting. It always makes me think. It reads, 'If not now, when?'.

If not now, when – for your relationship?

Because it can be very difficult to prioritize each other – particularly when you're settled together, and you've turned your attention from the excitement of winning each other to the routine of living with each other. You have to work ... do up the house ... ferry the kids round ... see friends ... visit family. The outside world can eat away at your relationship until there's almost nothing left.

So how can you stop it happening?

Make time for each other

Touch down at least every day, even if it's just for a quarter of an hour or so. Update each other on what's been happening. Talk through the problems. Build each other up for the next day ahead. Also, regularly spend longer periods with each other – a regular evening a week, a set weekend a month

Make that time one-to-one time

If when you're together you're also with your mates or your family, you won't make contact with each other – you'll be too busy seeing to their needs rather than to your own. So cancel the girls evening. Tell your Mum you'll see her next week. Give yourselves a chance to stare into each other's eyes without distractions.

Make that time quality time

Being together won't help if you're not really together. Yes of course relax and put your head in your partner's lap or vice versa. But don't just withdraw or sit side by side on the sofa practising your channel-hopping. Instead interact with each other, listening, talking, swapping notes, giving each other the experience of being happy together.

Spend time on your relationship, then your love will develop.

Don't spend the time, and it simply won't.

Whatever you put in the centre of your life is always the thing that grows most.

Read this if you want time away from him

When Ian and I decided to move in together, we wanted nothing more than to be with each other.

By that time, we both worked from home. And we had so little money that we didn't have much of a social life. So we never went out. We woke in the morning next to each other, had breakfast together, worked side by side in the same office, and snuggled up together every evening. It was incredibly, overwhelmingly romantic.

Except that looking back, we were very lucky we didn't strangle each other before the first month was out.

Yes, many couples don't realize they need to have time together. But many couples don't realize they've a right to want to be alone.

They work in a busy office all day, trek home on a crowded bus at night, spend the evening with the kids – and find themselves at the end of it all screaming for silence and a bit of personal space. In order to get that space, they then mysteriously find themselves snapping at their partner.

A good row may not clear the air. But it will at least clear the room.

If you live a life that's full of people, you may find yourself needing time alone – even from each other. Don't worry. It's a biological human necessity, so that you can recuperate mentally and emotionally. But the way humans live our lives nowadays, we typically don't get enough.

So be firm. Give yourselves time each day that is your

time. Even just a quarter of an hour to start thinking clearly again will do. Explain: 'I need some time alone to get my head sorted.' Reassure: 'I'm not upset or angry, there's nothing wrong – I just need some clear space.'

And then retreat: Go down the bottom of the garden. Go fishing. Pretend to be a teenager and lock yourself in your room. Sit on the loo with a book if necessary. (And support each other in this – don't disturb a partner who's taking sanity time.)

When you emerge, you'll be far more able to give the relationship the attention and love it deserves.

Ian and I? We learned the hard way. One evening three months in, the tension built to such an extent that he walked out, and I thought he was gone for good. Instead, he walked round the block – and an hour later, with his head cleared, came back bursting to tell me what he'd discovered.

'I think I know where we're going wrong,' he said. 'What we each need is a bit of time alone ...'

Read this if life gets just too much

If love seems hard, it may be life that's hard. Some everyday stresses and strains may mean that neither of you has any enthusiasm for giving, for sharing, for caring – or even for being civil to each other.

Here are four ongoing problems that, however much you love each other, will inevitably affect your relationship. They're physical conditions, but they'll also undermine you emotionally.

When you're tired all the time

The pace of life gets too hectic. There are too many demands, too many times when you're being tested, too many times when you have to prove yourself. You're exhausted and demoralized; you lash out daily at the one you love ...

... Take it seriously. Stress kills, literally and emotionally. So develop a healthier lifestyle, ease back on the work, the pressure, the desire to please. Make sure you have a good support network of family, friends and neighbours to help you cope with life. Read a good 'stress-busting' guide. Practise saying 'no' to requests and demands.

When you're ill

One of you is physically low and the ripples spread – to money worries; exhaustion from home nursing; anger at the situation. You start offloading your guilt and resentment on each other. You feel out of control – what if the problems just go on and on ...

... Don't try to cope alone. Get practical support, from medical professionals, support services, family, friends. Get emotional support, to reclaim a feeling of control over your lives and your future.

When you have a hormone imbalance

Menstruation, menopause, childbirth – plus medications such as HRT, the contraceptive pill and anabolic steroids. These things can turn a saint into a monster, and that monster's previously loving partner into a confused wreck.

... Get it sorted. Keep a diary of symptoms to track what's happening. Then work together to enrol your GP and/or alternative health practitioners in a recovery campaign.

When you're depressed

Depression bends reality. Through altered mental filters, the depressed person can see themselves as a failure, their partner a brute, the relationship a total trap. And then both of you may be tempted to head for the door.

... Sort it immediately. Anything more than two weeks of feeling low calls for action. See your GP and get counselling and advice. Don't be afraid to take medication – new types are not addictive and not for ever.

The key, though, is this. Don't take these things to heart. Yes sort them. But don't panic if while you're sorting them, the relationship goes to hell and back. The bad feelings will pass – the frustration, the depression, the fury ...

... and, the withdrawal. There'll be times in your life together when you'll each batten down the hatches, withdraw into yourselves and concentrate on survival – and this may mean you give each other no support, or even attention. Yes, of course if this is a way of life, challenge it. But if it's a fire-fighting response to an outside event, ride with it if you can.

And, if you can, ride with the natural fear that it will strike in you about your love. Keep trusting. Remember that up until now, you were fine together.

And remember that no one can keep on loving when it's taking all the energy they have just to keep going.

Read this if there's a sudden crisis

He's crashed the car. You've found a lump. (Or, of course, the other way round.)

Just sometimes, there'll be a crisis. And that will mean fear, anger and a lot of grief. It's useful to have a menu of possible strategies for when emergencies happen – because they'll put not only you, but also your relationship, under strain. Because love can be the first casualty of a crisis.

♥ Touch: Being held or cuddled comforts emotionally. Men in particular may prefer touch to talking because they can totally let go rather than having to perform or come up with solutions.

♥ Sex: Some people find sex an essential in times of crisis – releasing, relaxing, a statement of hope. Others turn off completely and think the whole idea is disgusting. Check out where you each are – don't assume. And if one of you needs it and the other doesn't, find an arrangement that works for both of you.

♥ Time to talk: Talking it all through resolves the feelings and clears the mind for action. So give each other space and time, encouragement and acceptance. Asking 'tell me more' questions such as, 'what happened then? ... how did you feel? ... what did you think?' will let you work things out of your system.

♥ Crying: Crying releases hormones that relax you and make you feel better. So let yourself cry – if your partner can't handle it, lock yourself in the bathroom. And give him support to cry – weeping is still sufficiently countercultural for a man that he'll need encouragement. See page 51 for ways to do this.

♥ Ranting: Getting angry may particularly be his preferred way of coping, because it raises energy, makes him feel in control – and it's more acceptable for a man than tears or panic. Of course veto harmful words or actions – but otherwise allow both of you a rant as a quick way to feel better. Again, see page 156 for helpful hints.

♥ Recuperation: After the initial crisis is over, take time together away from home – even just for a day. Take your minds off things completely, go shopping or sightseeing or walking. It may seem hardhearted. But it'll give your emotions and your brain a holiday and allow you to cope better when you come back.

♥ Get support: Welcome offers of help from friends, family or counsellors – not only for whoever's suffered the crisis directly, had the bereavement, or lost the job. The one of you who hasn't been directly in the firing line will need help too – first because they've been doing the caring, and second because they'll also have 'picked up' tension and stress from the main casualty.

♥ Practical action: Making plans and taking action makes you feel more in control. So when you know the extent of the crisis, gather your resources – supportive people, books, helplines or whatever – and get going. Be warned, though – feelings will still lurk even if you're solving the problem. So be prepared for emotional vulnerability for some time down the road.

♥ Focusing on the future: If there's been a disaster, hope always helps. Talking about how things may improve or looking at optimistic future possibilities will lift your mood. But don't try this too early, or it won't work. Sort out the present before you focus on the future.

Finally, remember that you'll have to customize.

Because what you want may not be what he needs. So if you offer and it's turned down, that's fine – instead, ask what would be better.

And, what he offers you may not be what you need. So if he offers and his offer is totally wrong, that's fine too. Instead, tell him what would be better.

Simple truth about love

In good times and in bad, you'll get a good relationship if you contribute equally.

But you'll get a better relationship if you value
contributions equally.

Don't always assume that what you give is worth
more than what he gives.

Or vice versa.

Read this if you argue over the money

Money can't buy you love. But it can destroy it.

Because here's an interesting statistic: 44 per cent of couples argue about money. Not whether they have a lot or a little – love can survive poverty just as well as luxury. But how exactly to spend what they have.

Why is all this so gut-wrenching? Why do so many couples say that their worst battles are about small green slips of paper?

We want what we want

Money gives us the power to have what we want. And we all want things. We want what feels right to us and in the way that feels right to us. Why should we give up what we want, even for the person we love?

We want our partners to give us what we want

On the other hand, we all want to know that the person we love will give up what they want for us. We all think that if our partner loved us, he'd agree that we should spend the money on what we want to spend it on. If he doesn't agree, then he doesn't love us enough.

We want what we're brought up to want

What we want to spend money on often springs from our childhood. If our parents allocated money only to essentials, then either we'll feel we should be thrifty, or we'll flip over and want to spend, spend, spend. Whichever, our way really feels the way 'things should be'. But if our partner was brought up differently, he'll have different ideas about 'the way things should be'. Trouble ahead.

We want what we want whether we earn the money or not

Traditionally, the deal's usually been that the partner who earns gets to say what money is spent on. And typically, 'he' earned, 'she' didn't. Now, typically he and she both earn, and in any case quite rightly money's seen as only one contribution to a partnership. At the moment, we're right in the middle of a shakedown in arrangements. Both partners feel they can make decisions whether they bring money in or not. Except that sometimes, if one partner suddenly stops earning, the earning partner conveniently forgets this, and starts arguing it all the traditional way.

We want to know we're OK whether we earn the money or not

Money may seem to be a problem because it's to do with power – power to have what we want. But there's a twist. Having money, having the power to spend money, also makes us feel good about ourselves. So if we don't get to spend money, or if we aren't earning money and therefore feel we can't choose how to spend it, we feel bad about ourselves.

When there's a money struggle in our partnership, we not only feel helpless. We also feel worthless.

Here are eight things to do that will help you sort out the power stuggles that make money problems so painful:

♥ Talk to each other about how your family managed money. Pinpoint the differences between you, then find out how these are causing problems.

♥ Try to understand that your spending patterns aren't necessarily right. Your partner's spending patterns aren't necessarily wrong. And, of course, vice versa.

♥ If you don't agree about money, go as far as you can without panicking to respect each other's way of doing things.

♥ If the two of you end up arguing about money, you'll both feel vulnerable – so add in extra reassurance, support and hugs to balance things out.

♥ Find a way to organize every money decision so that both of you get most of what you want most of the time.

♥ Make sure each of you has some money, even if only a bit, that you can spend exactly how you want, no questions, no objections.

♥ If one of you isn't earning for a while, remember that he or she will still be contributing. Money decisions have to reflect the fact that both of you have equal rights.

♥ Be aware that, actually, there is a limit to money. So sometimes, you may have to accept that you can't always have everything.

Read this if he won't help with the housework

When my friend Louise told me that her new partner 'didn't do housework', I have to admit I cringed.

She's a wonderful, assertive woman. How could she even think of pairing up with a man who didn't pull his weight around the house? She smiled and said, 'That's OK. I love the other parts of David. He does lots and lots of things that I can't or won't do; we divide the work of our relationship equally. And anyway, he might change.'

As their relationship grew deeper, as they got engaged, as they married and bought a house, I watched with interest to see whether Louise's prediction would come true. Because I have to say that it stuck in my throat that she was being so 'traditional'. And so calm. In survey after survey, picking up dirty socks and putting the top back on the toothpaste tube rate more highly than children and sex as argument topics. So why weren't Louise and David having blazing rows about it every night?

Because Louise hung in there. She didn't nag. She didn't blame. David had told her from the start that he didn't care what sort of state things were in and therefore didn't feel motivated to do housework – though if she wanted to, fair enough. She'd accepted that as part of the deal. And she stuck with it.

Except that, actually, the miracle happened. One day, after about a year of domestic perfection courtesy of Louise, she and David went to stay with friends. Friends who were doing up a half-demolished house, friends who were in no way domestic, friends who didn't believe in cleanliness or tidiness or clean sheets.

And the next morning, having spent a freezing damp night, and faced with a dirty and unhygienic bathroom, David cracked. He took a deep breath and suggested they leave. Now.

That evening, back home, he took the rubbish out. Louise gave him a round of applause.

From then on, David did housework.

The moral of this tale isn't that if you stay in half-built hovels, your partner will miraculously reform his lager lout habits. It's much deeper – and tougher – than that.

The first moral of this tale is that if you pair up with a man who's clear that housework isn't important to him, you're on a hiding to nowhere expecting him to do it. Sure, do the housework – but do it for yourself, in the way you want it done, because you want it done. Or, don't do the housework, and live with the consequences. Don't expect him to want it done, because he won't.

The second moral is that a good relationship is based on a division of labour that happily plays to your strengths and your weaknesses. David didn't do housework. But Louise didn't do lots of other things that were vital to their partnership. And she was happy it balanced itself out. Sometimes it works better if one of you does one set of tasks, and the other does the other. As long as you both carry equal weight, it doesn't matter which of you carries the feathers and which of you carries the lead.

Of course, absolutely don't submit with resentment to a divison of labour you feel is unfair. So if you both work, and if you then do 90 per cent of the work at home and he only does 10 per cent, make a stand. Make a stand calmly rather than angrily because otherwise he'll suddenly develop a hearing block. Make a stand clearly by writing out the support jobs that keep your partnership together, showing him the list, and then insisting on dividing them. And make a stand fairly – if he fills the car with petrol every week, that's just as much of a contribution as you putting the cat out every night. But do, for everyone's sake, make a stand.

The third and final moral of this tale is that a partner can learn. Not if you nag, not if you blame, not if you set standards so tight that he's bound to fail. And certainly not if every time he tries to learn to help around the house, you grab the iron from his hand, cast your eyes up to heaven and do it yourself. (All he'll learn from that is firstly that he's rubbish at ironing, and secondly that if he's rubbish enough, you'll do it for him.)

But if your partner gets to see how important housework is, and if you then give him a chance to do some, and if you then show him how pleased you are about it, then, like David did, he just might learn.

If he doesn't, then read on...

Read this if he really won't help with the housework

If all else fails, and your partner simply won't divide labour equally in your relationship, then there's one strategy that just might work.

It's risky, because it can destroy trust and good feeling. It may even blow your relationship out of the water.

But if you know that your relationship is on the line anyway, then you may want to try it. It has worked for other women, and it may work for you.

Quite simply, down tools.

Yes, look after your kids if you have them. But no, stop looking after your partner in whatever ways you feel he's taking you for granted. Until he reciprocates.

Only wash up when he does. Only cook when he does. Only iron when he does. Only do when he does.

And then hold firm while he tries to make you change your mind. While he sulks ... while he rants ... while he says you're being unreasonable, illogical and unfair.

In the end, he just might see reason, see logic, and play fair. In the end, he just might start working with you, cooperatively as an equal team.

It might just be worth a try...

Read this if a work event starts eroding your home life

Nowadays work's such a central part of life that it will always affect your relationship.

And it will sometimes destroy it.

That's particularly likely to happen when there's some sort of shift in your work situation – into it, out of it, upwards, downwards or sideways – that alters the contribution each of you are making.

Here are four work shifts that may start eroding your relationship – even if up to now it's been rock solid.

You go back to work

The kids are old enough and it's time to go back to work. But instead of more money and increased independence, what you get is a strained relationship. He starts complaining about your hours. You start feeling that you get more appreciation in the office than at home ...

Why? Well, when you spread your wings, you boost your confidence. And in comparison, your home life may start to seem boring and confining. In the meantime, your partner may not only resent not being looked after quite so full-time as before. He may also start fearing that you'll outgrow him and leave.

What can you do? You need to make sure you're both feeling secure. So make an extra effort to show your partner he's still the centre of your life. Share your work with him so that he feels involved and part of it. At the same time, encourage him to show you appreciation. And make particularly sure that the division of labour balances itself out – otherwise you'll add physical exhaustion to your emotional vulnerability (see pages 197 and 200).

One of you starts working at home

Freelance opportunity often means a home-based business. Sounds great – a more relaxed lifestyle and more time together. But all of a sudden you may be tripping over each other round the house. And there's friction about whether working from home actually means skiving off – and so should be taken less seriously.

Why? Well, when one (or both) of you starts using your home space for business space, that's the signal for territory wars. You both feel invaded as work demands intrude on house space, or home responsibilities eat away at working time. The homeworker may also feel that their labours are seen as somehow less important.

What can you do? The secret here is to draw clear demarcations. Allocate one room to work, and don't let it spill out. Allocate set hours to work and don't let them spill over.

But also, see the homeworker as a real worker, not someone who can always be relied on to slot several hours of house cleaning into their professional working day. If necessary, get dressed as if to go to the office and work a strict nine to five.

One of you loses their job

Redundancy, relocation, or even a sacking. The professional impact's cruel, both financially and emotionally. But you may not expect that it hits your relationship too. So that at the very time you need to be supporting each other, you actually end up tearing each other apart ...

Why? Well, job loss not only means a loss of confidence. It can also mean a loss of control – because bringing home the money may go hand in hand with having a say in the decision making. Add to this the very different day-to-day deal when a worker has to stay at home, even if only for a while, and you have a recipe for disaster.

What can you do? If it's your partner who's lost his job, then keep reassuring him that he's still valuable, and that you still love him. If it's you, then do all you can to bolster your own confidence and get your partner to help you in that.

Restructure your lives so that whoever's now at home full-time doesn't cause day to day friction – and maybe even takes responsibility and makes extra contribution to the running of the house.

Particularly, avoid the temptation to alter the balance of power. A non-earning partner should still have equal rights because they're an equal partner.

One of you has a success

There's a promotion, a rise, an exciting new responsibility. But when the celebration dinner's over, things turn sour. The less successful one of you starts having problems – illness, work crisis, temper tantrums. The successful one starts to feel undermined – at just the time when the stress is proving too much ...

Why? Well, competition and love don't mix. So if one of you feels upstaged – particularly if they've previously always been top dog – they may get envious, lose confidence, feel less valuable in the relationship. So then they try to rebalance things by grabbing attention, or by criticizing the other's success. Not surprisingly, the successful one resents that.

What can you do? The successful partner needs to keep clearly in mind how valuable they are at home and at work. The upstaged one needs to keep a lid on their wetblanket feelings.

Because in the work arena, as in everything else, loving your partner means being happy for their success, not envious.

Remember that the victory belongs to both of you, because you are a partnership.

Simple truth about love

You can call it passion. You can call it eroticism. You can call it sex.

But if you call it making love, you're double accurate.

Because making love isn't just what it is.

It's also what it does.

Read this if you haven't slept together in living memory

I overheard this one, but I wasn't deliberately eavesdropping. I was having dinner with a friend in a favourite Italian restaurant, and half way through the evening, in walked a group of about half a dozen women who had obviously come straight from a late session at work.

They took the table next to us, immediately ordered three carafes of red wine, and then kept it pouring. They were obviously tired, a bit loud, a bit giggly, and by the time we were on our pud, the next three carafes were going down nicely.

And then the dark-haired one in the red dress burst into tears.

Someone gave her a cuddle, and someone else passed over the hankies, and everyone asked what was the matter. The weeper sniffed and blew her nose and said, in a voice sufficiently loud that I could hear it without straining ...

'I don't know what's wrong. I don't know what to do ... We're ...We've ... We only sleep together twice a week now – and it used to be every night!'

At which point, everyone cracked up laughing. When they'd got their breath back, three women at once started telling her that nothing was wrong ... that this was normal. And that if they were still sleeping together twice a week, then she was a luckier woman than most.

I listened and I felt so sorry for her. But I wasn't at all surprised that she'd cracked as she had.

Of all the problems couples suffer around sex, the most

usual's just not having it. My bet is that if you took a (truthful) head count round any restaurant – or workplace, or cinema, or shopping mall – you'd find that most of the couples who've been together more than a few years aren't making love as much as they used to. And not nearly as much as they'd like to.

So if you're in the same situation as the woman in the restaurant, you're not alone.

But you may be completely confused about what to do. The reasons you're not sleeping together can be so complex that they can seem like one of those convoluted murder mysteries. Did it start when he went on night shift ... or when the baby arrived ... with that world-ending row ... or with that big project at work that made sex the last thing on your mind?

But as in a murder mystery, it is possible to track down and solve the problem of why you're not making love any more. Through motive, means and opportunity ...

Opportunity

To have sex, you need the opportunity to have sex. You have to have the time and space to simply do it.

You probably don't have that opportunity. There aren't that many hours in the day. Or, there may not be the space – particularly if you have children who're likely to walk into your bedroom completely unannounced. The best contraceptive in the world is a three-year-old who hasn't yet grasped the point of sleeping.

So set aside prime time. Book it in. Take a whole evening for sex each week rather than just the quarter of an hour before you fall asleep. Go away for the weekend rather than trying to juggle home life and sex life together. You may spend the first three dedicated evenings or weekends just sleeping. But gradually, you'll catch up and start making use of the opportunity you're giving yourself.

Means

To have sex, you need the means to have sex. In other words, you need to get turned on in the first place, and then let each other know you're turned on.

Sometimes the turn on simply never happens any more. You love each other, you feel comfortable with each other. But aroused? Excuse me?

This is particularly likely if you haven't had sex for a while, and every time you think of it, you get nervous and embarrassed, and your mental circuits close down. So start being romantic again. Overcome the nervousness and embarrassment with sheer good feeling about each other and confidence in the relationship.

Another twist is that you get turned on, but don't tell each other. You're scared of getting rejected. Or you've lost that set of nonverbal signals that originally meant 'let's have sex'. So make it more obvious when you want him.

And, be willing to at least give it a go when he makes it obvious that he wants you – if you're really not getting turned on after five minutes, then say stop. But sometimes moving just slightly towards sex can create the arousal you need in order to go all the way.

Also, use fantasy. It's not a betrayal of your love – and it is a wonderful engine-starter. So talk about what you want to do to each other, spin stories of ideal sex, talk about the best time you've ever had together. If your bodies won't slide easily into a sexual gear, use your minds to make the connection.

Motive

To have sex, you need a motive to have sex. You have to be able to imagine there being something worthwhile once you've got past that initial foreplay.

So most basically, make sure that you – as well as him – are having an orgasm. You may never have had one. Or, you may have had them in the past, but not any more because foreplay's got shorter and shorter. If so, your body may not quite see the point of lovemaking. So find out – or rediscover – how you need to make love so you both climax most of the time.

Also, update each other on what turns you on. Tastes change and so do nerve endings, and what was a turn on for both of you when you were first together may now be just routine or irrelevant. So do a regular inventory of 'what do I really like ... what would really turn you on ...'. Or swap one request – not complaint – every time you do start getting physical.

Lovemaking also has to motivate emotionally. If you don't feel appreciated, trusted and trusting, then you won't feel like sex. The most effective aphrodisiac is telling each other that you still love and like, not only that you lust.

There's a final warning. You need body, mind and emotions to all work together to get a failing sex life back. Because passion isn't stupid – it can tell when some part of you isn't really interested or committed. So it won't work just to bolt on silly costumes or wacky new techniques for the sake of it. And it might even be necessary to get professional help to overcome your problems, particularly emotional ones – seething resentment and erotic fulfilment aren't good bedfellows.

But if you want the sex back and are prepared to prioritize getting it back, then you'll almost certainly succeed.

Resuscitating dead passion can feel impossible. But it can be done.

Read this if every day's a bad sex day

There'll always be the occasional bad sex day. You need to expect it, ride it, take it in your stride.

But what if every day's a bad sex day?

What if there are problems that stop you having sex, stop you enjoying sex, stop you bringing sex to a positive climax?

Here are seven typical ones:

- ♥ He can't get an erection.
- ♥ You find sex uncomfortable or painful.
- ♥ He can get an erection but can't keep it.
- ♥ You can't get a climax.
- ♥ He comes too quickly.
- ♥ You can't bear penetration.
- ♥ He doesn't come at all.

The strange thing is that if bad sex days are the norm, the temptation to carry on as usual is almost overwhelming. We wouldn't tolerate a broken washing machine for more than an hour or two. But when it comes to sex we'll carry on regardless for weeks, months, maybe even years.

Because we think that sex is something we ought to be able to sort out on our own – if we can't, we're sad. Or we think that no one else could sort out our sexual problems – and so we don't bother asking. Or we hang back through an embarrassment that paralyses, or through a love that doesn't want to make waves.

We hope against hope that magically one night we'll turn

to each other and everything will be perfect again.

But it doesn't often happen like that. Sometimes you need more than hope.

You may need physical intervention

Is there a physical cause to what's happening? This is particularly likely if the problem started suddenly, and doesn't seem to be linked to anything upsetting that's happened to you or between the two of you.

If so, go to your GP and get him or her to give you a medical checkup. If there's a physical problem, condition or infection, get treatment. If it's medication that's creating the difficulty, find out if you can change to another medication that doesn't have those side effects.

You may need information

Is your problem down to lack of facts or expertise? This is particularly likely if the problem's always been there, and hinges around lack of fulfilment – such as one or both of you being unable to climax.

If so, buy a good sex manual – there are some suggestions in the back of the book. These manuals can often also talk you through practical exercises to help you develop the knowledge and skills you missed out on.

You may need emotional support

Has the problem been triggered by emotions? This is particularly likely if sex brings up strong negative feelings for one or both of you, or has been triggered by an upsetting emotional event – a row, an affair, a bereavement, or even a traumatic past event such as sexual abuse or rape.

If so, you may get your feelings sorted simply by talking through the event with each other so that you lay it to rest. More likely you'll need expert help from a counsellor – there are some useful addresses in the back of the book.

If you need any more encouragement to get help right away, then let me tell you the story of Elizabeth.

She wrote to me as an agony aunt a few years ago, explaining that her husband found it difficult to make love. Specifically, he could last perhaps thirty seconds and that was it. She was 60 and he was 62 – and as she explained the relationship was beginning to get a bit strained.

As I read her letter, I mentally rehearsed my reply – how I would explain the possible medical causes of this problem, suggest some sex therapy exercises, finish with a reassuring paragraph about hanging on in there.

And then I read the ps. which said ... 'We've had this problem since the day we married 35 years ago, and have only twice achieved proper penetration. I've never dared tell anyone – it's not the sort of thing you talk about. But we're getting old, and it would be so nice to get it sorted.'

And it would be so nice to report that I was able to write back. To offer Elizabeth the emotional support and the practical help that that I so desperately wanted to give and that she'd so desperately needed for over a third of a century.

But in her embarrassment, Elizabeth had totally forgotten to include her return address.

Simple truth about love

Love may start with you clinging together for dear life.

But if you carry on clinging together, you'll see your relationship dying.

As the proverb says, love isn't just two people gazing inward at each other.

It's two people looking outward yet in the same direction.

---

love coach

Read this if the baby's born and everything's falling apart

This story happened to a woman I'm very fond of. But I'm sure it's also happened, millions of times, to thousands of other women too.

When Julie learned she was pregnant, she and Rob were completely over the moon. A happy marriage, a lovely flat, a longed-for baby. What more could they want? The pregnancy went well, the labour went well enough for a first time, and as she woke the next morning, still exhausted but with baby Jake beside her, Julie felt that life had never been so complete.

Things went downhill from then on.

The first thing, of course, was the exhaustion. She was still recovering from labour. And the four-hourly feeds – not to mention Jake's habit of crying all night – meant she got very little sleep. She felt she had no energy for anything except the baby, and her whole life had slowed down to a snail's pace.

She also felt trapped. Actually, she was trapped. Jake's cries dictated everything she did. And it gradually dawned on Julie that for the next decade, minimum, she just wasn't free to go out when she wanted to, to sleep when she wanted to, even to drink a good bottle of wine when she wanted to. What she needed was just a little bit of space and time to call her own. No way. She had to be completely in control of herself and her life all the time.

She and Rob supported each other where they could. But she was so focused on the baby that she didn't have much time left for Rob. And he had night shift to do.

He felt sidelined. She felt unsupported. They couldn't even row and clear the air because that woke Jake up again.

Seven weeks to the day that the baby was born, Julie got up at two o'clock one morning to feed him. But after he was fed, he didn't calm down. Instead he screamed. And screamed. And screamed. Alone with him in their eighth floor flat, she held him as he yelled. Walked up and down with him as he howled.

And in a sudden clear moment, Julie realized that there was a very simple answer to all her problems. An answer that would free her up to live the life she wanted. And free their relationship up to be happy again.

All she had to do was to open the window. Throw the baby out. Close the window. And go back to bed.

When Rob came in half an hour later, he found Julie sitting on the floor in tears. She hadn't done what she thought of doing. But she knew – and she'll always know – that it was a very close thing.

Because yes, having a baby is wonderful. It's a statement of commitment, a proof of your love. When you've got the hang of it, then it can be the most wonderful project you'll ever undertake in your whole life. But it will never be easy – and once it's started, there's no going back.

So expect that having children – particularly having your first child – is going to trigger immense strains in your relationship, strains that will test all your love and commitment to the limit. Don't try to carry on as normal. Do try everything you can to ease the problems.

Get good support practically

When baby's born, get medical help to sort problems such as post-labour exhaustion and post-natal depression.

As baby grows, remember that caring for him (or her) is a demanding job physically and emotionally – so get as much practical support as you can. Rope in friends, family, health visitors and anyone else that you can call up. Get them to take over and give you some time out. A sane parent is a good parent. One who's half out of her (or his) mind with sleep deprivation isn't.

Also, learn from your support people; you aren't expected to know what to do in every situation. On the other hand, don't get put off by everyone telling you what to do. They'll 'should' you to death; if you get overwhelmed, don't argue. Just nod, agree, then trust your own instincts to do exactly what is best for your own child.

Fight feeling trapped

Having children is a commitment of at least two decades. So expect that at some point early in the proceedings you'll feel trapped – literally and emotionally – by that fact. Don't give yourself a hard time if, though you love your baby dearly, you will sometimes wish he or she had never been born.

To help offset those feelings, do all you can to give yourselves some basic freedoms. The freedom to have a one-to-one adult conversation – even if that means popping the baby in its cot while you give each other attention. The freedom to have some time to yourselves – even if that means getting a baby-sitter and going for a walk. The freedom to spend some money on yourselves, even if it's only a few pounds, without feeling guilty that you're not spending it on the baby.

Be parents and lovers together

Yes, you're both parents. But you're both also still partners.

If you feel you're a mother rather than a lover, it won't be any wonder if you never want sex. And if the baby is always the centre of your attention, it'll be no wonder if your partner feels put out. So major on all the romantic bits that remind each other that you're still sexual – evening meals together, gazing into eyes, and cuddling up on the sofa. Make an effort to reassure each other not only that you still love but that you also lust.

And that you can put that lust into practice. Even if it feels a bit strange, make love as soon as you get the medical all clear. And read through all the tips on page 198 for how to reclaim a disappearing sex life – in order to make sure that yours makes a full comeback after the birth.

One last tip. Parentline PMS and National Stepfamily Association is a charity that support parents in all aspects of childcare, particularly if you're under stress. It runs support groups and has a daily helpline. The number is 08088 002222. If you're feeling under strain because of parenthood, ring that number now.

Read this if you keep rowing over the kids

One day last spring I was sitting on a park bench reading. And just in front of me on the grass was a little boy – aged four or maybe five.

On the next bench along from me were his parents. They were great with the little one. Every few minutes, the mother would call the little boy back to her. When he arrived, his father would throw the ball, or encourage him to chase the pigeons.

In between times, I couldn't help noticing, they were having the most almighty row with each other.

I don't know the details. It was about the child, and the way he was growing up, and the way he should behave. The details were irrelevant. The point was that they disagreed in what they believed about the little boy. And that they each felt so passionately about what they believed that it hurt. I felt for both of them. That little boy was very loved.

Suddenly, the whole thing fell apart. She turned away sharply. He stood up suddenly. And as I listened, their voices rose, so that I heard clearly their last words to each other:

She said, 'He's our son. Our son!'

And he said, 'Yes, he is. But you wouldn't think it. You just don't let me even try to be his father. Fine. As you like.' And he walked away.

I heard what that man said, and I knew what he meant. Because though loving each other is important, loving your children tears at your heart strings. To protect them you'd put your life on the line. And you'd put your partnership on the line.

So if you think your partner is wrong in his childrearing ideas, you'll override him – because your children have to have the best. And for your children, you think you know best.

Often, you do know best. As a woman, the chances are that you've simply had more experience of kids; you've done more baby-sitting; you've watched your aunties and cousins and colleagues and friends with their toddlers. And as your children's mother, you've carried them, given birth to them, and probably spent anything up to quadruple the time with them that your partner has.

So when his ideas about caring for your children clash with your ideas about caring for your children, you turn mother tiger. Anything rather than do less than the best for your cubs.

What you're doing is well-intentioned. And it's often right. But may I offer you a warning, passed on to me by many mothers and grandmothers over the years? Your mother tiger act is also, sometimes, dangerous.

Because either you'll both hang in there getting more and more extreme in your attitudes. Or, your partner will learn the lesson you're so desperately teaching him – that he's getting it wrong.

But rather than hanging in there and trying to get it right, he may just opt out – as the father in the park did – and let you take over. He'll stand back, see his children slipping away from him. And pretty soon, he'll slip away from them, too.

If you and your partner have different ideas about bringing up your children, then instead of seeing them as alternatives, see them as combinable options.

Remember that you're not the only parent

They're his children as well as yours – he has a right to input (though see my ps. on step-parents). And, your way isn't necessarily the right way just because you're the children's mother – he is, after all, their father. So don't exclude. Include and accept his ideas and approaches – there'll be more similarity and more crossover than you think. Then discuss together ways of combining your approaches.

Remember that orders don't motivate

A father who's 'told' to treat his children a particular way won't just feel resentful or patronized. He'll also, probably without meaning to, undermine the way he's been told to act. If you explain to your partner why you do what you do, he'll be far more likely to follow through on that. He'll also be more likely to learn from it and start treating the children in the way you do.

Remember he may have to learn

If you want your partner to become a good father, then he has to develop the skills. And all skill development happens through trial and error. Of course keep an eye on things. Of course step in if he's going to do something actively dangerous. But don't monitor and criticize everything he does – to learn, he needs to make a few mistakes along the way.

Remember to value his contribution

His ways of parenting, have their value – there is a 'Daddy' way of doing it as well as a 'Mummy' way. He'll have gained ideas and values from his upbringing that are useful to your children. And though you need to present a united front on many things, it's also good for children to have more than one option and more than one role model in life.

love coach

(Ps: It may be, of course, that you are the children's biological parent, and your partner isn't. If so, then adapt what I'm saying here to take into account the length and commitment of your relationship with him.

But remember that if you've given your partner any responsibilities in caring for your children as part of his love for you, then whatever his blood relationship to them, he has some rights in this situation. And also that the more you enrol him in what's happening, the better the parenting your children will receive.)

Read this if a midlife crisis stirs things up

When an old friend and I drove up together from London to Liverpool, I thought it was going to be a relaxed and uneventful journey.

Silly me.

Somewhere around Watford Gap, Martin started talking about what was really bothering him. Which was that he'd come to a fork in the road.

The last of his daughters had just left home. His boss had hinted there was no point in applying for promotion again. The mortgage was nearly up on his house. So this was his chance of escape – move on, sell up, maybe just hang out, maybe just up and go.

It would have been nice to wave him on his way with an envious smile. There was just one problem.

Martin's wife, Gill .

Not her fault that she adored the village they lived in, that she wanted to be near the girls, that her first grandchild was on the way. And that the last thing she wanted in her late fifties was to up and leave everything she loved.

Everything? Well yes, they'd had their problems lately. So perhaps it was as good a time as any to make the break ...

Lots of couples reach this point, a midlife plateau where life is good, but you're ready to go in a different direction. It may be triggered by a single event – your children leaving, your grandchild being born, even your parents dying. It may be triggered by a trend – a levelling out of career achievement, the menopause, or simply a feeling of stagnation where there used to be an urge to move on.

These are the three most typical reactions to a midlife stage:

♥ Panic makes you act younger. You rediscover sex or drugs, or even rock and roll. You rebel and kick over the traces – and that might include your relationship.
♥ Weariness makes you act older. You give up things you always found a struggle, such as achieving, giving or loving. With a sigh of relief, you retreat into your nest.
♥ Despair makes you give up. You believe that now you've nothing left to do. You feel useless and depressed. You give up on sex and love. Almost, you give up on life.

Typically, as with Martin and Gill, one partner hits all this first, and often overnight shifts their entire attitude to life. The other's left wondering what's happened, why their partner is suddenly living life in the fast lane, or the slow lane.

If you have a midlife crisis, and you want your relationship to survive, then that's usually possible. But you need to act, to reclaim a lot of things that you used to have and use them in the future you're facing. (And if it's your partner who's having the midlife crisis, then you need to be patient and supportive while he does this.)

You need to get back your belief in yourself

If you've always seen your main value in life as a parent or a worker, and if at midlife the children have left or the job's gone stale, you may panic.

But in fact you've almost certainly got another thirty-plus years ahead to reinvent who you are and get back your sense of importance. There are no rules – nothing that says you can't retrain, or get a job, or get a new job, or be a sex object, or whatever you want to do.

(If it's your partner who's going through a midlife crisis, support him as much as you can in whatever new directions he wants to take to help him feel important again.)

You need to get back your belief in each other

You've probably lost touch with each other over the years – too much time spent talking about nappies and school runs, or not talking because of the pressures of work.

So take the time and make the time to rediscover each other. It won't happen overnight. You're going to have to have conversations that you haven't had the opportunity for in the last two decades. Find out what he thinks, what he feels, what he wants out of life now. In return, tell him these things about you.

(If it's your partner who's going through a midlife crisis, aim to give him the sense that you see him as a partner and a lover, not just a spouse and a parent. If you can, he'll find it easier to see you that way too.)

You need to get back your belief in your relationship

You may need to reinvent your love – but you can do that.

You can make new goals to replace the previous goal of bringing up your children or developing your career. You can make new commitments, to have fun, to travel, to get a sex life back. You can start from scratch, deliberately setting aside everything that brought you together, and making new agreements on what's expected, and what's allowed.

(If it's your partner who's going through a midlife crisis, be flexible about the future. If he's changing, his goals may change – go with him as far down the road as you can, and together try to build a new life plan that suits both of you.)

Martin and Gill, by the way, are still together. He's retired and is doing voluntary work. She's helping to look after the grandchildren, but they travel a lot as well. They both gave up things in order to stay together – but they gained things too.

Last time I drove Martin back up from London to Liverpool, I wondered if it was going to be another journey full of worries and unhappiness.

He talked about football the whole way up. And that was fine by me.

Read this if things are changing and you're scared

One of the highlights of my life was my first visit to St Petersburg – or Leningrad as it was then. And one of the highlights of that visit was seeing the frozen River Neva, a river so solidly frozen that it was possible to walk across it.

The last night we were there, at two o'clock in the morning, my friend Clive and I did just that.

We clambered down from the snowy promenade, under a yellow and icy sky, pulled our coats more tightly round us and set off across the river. Seeing the lights on the far side. Trembling with cold and excitement.

When we reached about half way, we stopped, and turned a slow full circle to see both sides of the river and left and right along its length. Heavy, gunmetal sky overhead, shadowy buildings and twinkling lights each side. Under our feet, solid ice.

And then we turned back. Knowing that we'd done it. Crossed the river. Braved our fears. Walked on water.

The next day, just before we left for the airport, Clive and I walked out from the hotel for one last look at our scene of victory. As we reached the promenade, and leaned over the railing, we were stopped in our tracks.

The ice had melted.

In the last twelve hours, just since the previous night, everything had changed. The rushing waters of the River Neva, which had been flowing below the ice all during the winter months, had finally broken through. So where there had been ice, there were now ice flows. And where there had been solidity under our feet, there were now vast stretches of running river.

We hadn't been aware of it the previous night, but we knew now that it had all been happening underneath us. And that while yesterday we'd been able to walk on water, if we wanted to cross the river today, we'd have to do something very different ...

If you get the sense that something has altered in your relationship, that your partner is somehow changed, or that the deal you had has somehow shifted, then it may well have done.

Because everything changes ... and so do you ... and so does your partner. And sometimes that melts the ground from under your feet.

Yes, it's tempting to believe that in love you remain stable, that love guarantees stability, and that you'll stay the same lovers that you always were.

But though the man you woke up next to this morning may look the same as the man you originally made a commitment to – plus or minus a few grey hairs – inside, he's changed, in big ways and in little ones. And so have you.

Over your relationship, even if no big events seem to have happened or no crucial life stages passed, you will inevitably alter. If nothing else, the relationship itself – the interactions you've had with each other – will have changed you. The deal you started your relationship with may not be the deal you have even a few years on

Ideals may have become pragmatic – or more idealistic. Goals may have been scaled down – or up. You may have started to value different things – companionship rather than lust, commitment rather than excitement. You will have altered your attitude to work, to kids, to friends, to family. You may have begun to expect different things of each other, or of the relationship.

And not always for the best.

Your partner may have become more of who you like. But he might have become less. You may have become more of who he likes. Or less. As a couple, you may have become more compatible, more solid. Or, you may be very different now and the relationship may be starting to melt beneath you. And if it is, then you'll need all your love and courage to keep things together.

If you, your partner or your relationship are changing or have changed, the first step is to realize it's normal. This happens, can't not happen. What you have to do is navigate through it.

So keep communicating. Stay in step with the ways each of you is altering your views, your feelings, your attitudes. If you can keep understanding each other, then however much you alter, your love will either stay the same or increase.

Particularly, tell each other how your expectations have changed. What you want and need from each other now may not be what you wanted and needed before. If you don't update on what you now expect fron the relationship, you'll fail to meet each other's expectations and you'll get disillusioned.

And give it time. Change is most upsetting in the early stages, when you're not quite sure what's happening, and you're afraid that it will hurt. Over weeks, months and years, you'll start to appreciate the alterations in your partner and in you – and to cope with them.

Finally, remember that it may seem as if the people you were, and the relationship you had, are the only good ones because they were the first ones ...

But the relationship you grow into – even if it involves new values, new feelings and new beliefs – may be even more worthwhile than the one you used to have. So go with it.

Very soon, you may love the person your partner has become even more than you loved the person he originally was.

And you may be even happier in your new relationship than you were in the old one.

Read this if you want a final bit of motivation

Inside every love relationship isn't only the promise of happy partnership.

There's also the promise of more effective, more developed, more fulfilled partners.

Because love is an arena where you get a lot of experience, a lot of opportunities to learn, to grow, to develop. Through the easy bits of love – the feeling good about each other ... the getting what you need ... the good sex ... the brilliant communication.

But also, through the painful bits – the feeling bad about each other and working through that ... the giving what your partner needs and smiling through that ... the sex that goes off the boil and needs attention ... the communication that stutters to a halt and needs renewed commitment. All these are ways of growing as well as ways of loving.

Yes, love's hard, and it often hurts. But if you make it work, it doesn't only mean you get the happiness and contentment that a good relationship brings you. It doesn't only mean that you get to have more of what you want.

It also means that you get to be more of who you want to be. In a relationship that really works, you get to be a better person, more understanding, more tolerant, less power-hungry, more accepting, more flexible, more able to be happy in your life and make others happy in theirs.

The bottom line is this. If you love each other, then you'll both be more able to love yourselves.

If you develop in your partnership, then you'll both develop in yourselves.

And if your relationship grows to be the best it can be ...

... then you'll both grow to be the best you can be, too.

Simple truth about love 20

Here's the bad news.

Learning to love never comes to an end.

Because there are always new challenges to face, new problems to solve, new skills to be mastered.

But actually, when you face those challenges, solve those problems, master those skills, you'll find things are better than ever.

The more you learn to love, the happier you'll be.

And so here's the good news.

Learning to love never comes to an end.

Read this if you feel you need more support

While reading this book, you may have realized that what's happening in your relationship – outside stresses, or internal conflicts – isn't something that you and your partner can cope with on your own. If so, well done for realizing it. Now get yourselves some help.

This section lists your options. It explains where you can go for support, and includes the names, addresses, numbers and websites of useful organizations.

Your GP

If either of you has physical or mental health problems, then these will be affecting your relationship. Your GP practice can offer medical help and a wide variety of support services such as stress management.

Though GP practices don't usually offer relationship counselling, they do usually have their finger on the pulse of local counselling services and can put you in touch. If you're not sure of the name or address of your doctor, try the Yellow Pages under D.

Your work support system

If you work, then your employer's personnel or human resources officer may be able to help with any practical or emotional problems you're having. Many firms offer counselling as part of the work package, and this often includes relationship counselling, face-to-face or via a helpline. If they don't offer this, they'll certainly be able to put you in touch with a local counsellor.

In both cases, it's wise to warn your employer if you're having relationship problems that may be affecting your work. That way they know what's happening and can be more sympathetic and supportive. If you're worried about everyone in your workplace knowing your problem, you can ask to keep things confidential.

Helplines

If you have a specific medical or practical problem that's affecting your relationship, there's usually a helpline to cover it. You can pick up the phone and speak to someone right away for information, advice and suggestions for local treatment or counselling.

Here are a selection of helplines addressing problems that may put strain on relationships:

♥ **National Association of CAB**: Helpline for the nearest branch check in your phone book under 'C' or Yellow Pages under 'Counselling and Advice'

♥ **National Debtline**: Helpline 0645 500511 (10am–4pm Monday and Thursday, 10am-7pm Tuesday and Wednesday, 10am-midday Friday)

♥ **Drinkline**: Helpline 0800 917 8282 (9am–11pm weekdays and 6pm-11pm weekends)

♥ **National Drugs Helpline**: Helpline 0800 776600 (24 hour)

♥ **Child Death Helpline**: Helpline 0800 282986 (10am–1pm Monday,

Wednesday and Friday, 7pm_10pm every day)

- ♥ **Carers National Association**: Helpline 0808 808 7777 (10am–midday, 2pm–4pm weekdays)
- ♥ **Shelter**: Helpline 0808 800 4444 (24 hour)
- ♥ **MIND**: Helpline 0181 522 1728 – Info Line 0345 660163 (9.15am–4.45pm weekdays)
- ♥ **Parentline PMS and National Stepfamily Association UK**: Helpline 08088 002222 (9am–9pm Monday – Saturday)

When it comes to relationship problems, helplines don't typically offer trained or long-term support. So it's usually better to see a counsellor face to face. But these helplines will be able to help you plan your next step.

- ♥ **Relate and The Sun Liveline**: 09069 123715 open 9am–10pm every day; calls cost £1.00 per minute and are limited to twenty minutes per caller
- ♥ **Jewish Marriage Council**: Helpline 0345 581999 open 9am–5pm weekdays
- ♥ **Marriage Care**: Catholic Marriage Advisory Council: Helpline 0345 573921 open 3pm-9pm Monday and Thursday
- ♥ **You Magazine and Mail on Sunday Relationships**: Helpline 0171 938 7577 open 11am–3pm Mondays (except Bank Holidays)

Some helplines are better than others. If you're concerned about quality, the Telephone Helplines Directory – from your local library or on website http://www.helplines.org.uk – gives you a list of all helplines that subscribe to a quality code of practice.

Counselling

You may decide to see a counsellor who will see one or both of you to work out your problems.

For counselling on general problems, your GP is your best starting point. You can also contact the British Association for Counselling 01788 578328 (24 hour information anwerphone) for a list of counsellors in your area. The Voluntary Agencies Directory, available in your local library, also lists contact details for the bigger specialized counselling organizations, who can then refer you on to support in your area. And all the helplines mentioned above will typically have listings of national and local counselling agencies that they can give you over the phone.

For relationship problems, the national organization Relate has local branches round the country. They offer counselling and sex therapy to help with problems in any adult couple relationship, married or unmarried, heterosexual or homosexual. You don't have to both go – they are happy to see just one of you. For details contact 01788 573241 or write to Relate at Herbert Gray College, Little Church Street, Rugby, Warwickshire, CV21 3AP

There are several other relationship guidance organizations that focus on particular groups.

- ♥ **Jewish Marriage Council**: 23 Ravenshurst Avenue, London NW4 4EE. Helpline: 0345 581999 (9am–5pm weekdays)
- ♥ **Marriage Care** (Catholic Marriage Advisory Council): 1 Blythe Mews, Blythe Road, London W14 0NW. Helpline: 0345 573921 (3pm–9pm Monday and Thursday)
- ♥ **Couple Counselling Scotland**: 105 Hanover Street, Edinburgh

EH2 1DJ. Tel: 0131 225 5006 (9am-4.30pm Monday to Thursday, 9am–4pm Friday)

♥ **London Lesbian and Gay Switchboard**: PO Box 7324, London, N1 9QS. Helpline: 0171 837 7324 (24 hour)

The Samaritans

If you need to talk confidentially to someone about your relationship at any time of the day or night, call The Samaritans. You don't have to be thinking of suicide – they'll help anyone who needs to talk through their feelings, and will also usually have a list of resources in your area.

♥ Ring 0345-909090 (1850-609090 in the Republic of Ireland) 24 hours a day 365 days a year, for the cost of a local call.
♥ Ring your local Branch direct- the number will be in the phone book.
♥ If you're deaf or hard of hearing, ring 08457-909192.
♥ Write to Chris, The Samaritans, PO Box 90 90, Slough Sl1 1UU
♥ Use email: Jo@samaritans.org or samaritans@anon.twwells.com if you want your email to remain anonymous.

America

Useful help organizations:

♥ The Family Care Giver Alliance: 425 Bush Street, Suite 500, San Francisco, CA 94108. Helpline: (415) 434 3388
♥ American Associations of Marriage and Family Therapy: 1133 Fifteenth Street, NW 3300, Washington DC, 20005-2710. Helpline: (202) 452 0109. Website: www.aamft.org (useful website for finding accredited counselor/therapist)

- ♥ Step Family Association of America Inc.: 650 J Street, Suite 205, Lincoln, NE 68508. Helpline: (800) 735 0329
- ♥ National Coalition for the Homeless: 1012 Fourteenth Street, NW 600, Washington DC 20005-3410. Helpline: (202) 737 6444
- ♥ Samaritans of Cape Cod: PO Box 65, Falmouth, MA 02540. Helpline: (508) 548 8900
- ♥ National Gay and Lesbian Task Force: 1700 Kalorama Rd NW, Washington DC, 20009-2624. Tel: (202) 332 6483

Australia

Useful help organizations:

- ♥ Centre for Education and Information on Drugs and Alcohol CIDA: PMB No. 6, Rozelle, NSW 2039. Helpline: 02 9818 0444. 24 Hour Drug and Alchohol Line 02 9361 2111
- ♥ Compassionate Friends Bereaved Parent Centre*: 267 Canterbury Road, Canterbury, Melbourne, Victoria 3126. Helpline: 03 9888 4944 (24 hour).
- ♥ Carers Association of Australia*: PO Box 3717, Weston, ACT 2611. Helpline: 02 6288 4877.
- ♥ Shelter NSW Co-op Ltd*: Suite 2, Fourth Floor, 307-383 Sussex Street, Sydney, NSW 2000. Helpline 02 9267 5733.
- ♥ Gay and Lesbian Counselling of NSW: 197 Albion Street, Surrey Hills, NSW. Helpline 02 9207 2888. Counsellor helpline 02 9207 2800.
- ♥ Samaritan Befrienders*: PO Box 991, Albany, WA 6330. Helpline 08 9842 2776.

These organizations have a centre in every state. Please contact the number above to find your nearest centre.

Books

These books cover specific problems that may be affecting your relationship

Sweet, Corinne. *Overcoming Addiction*, Piatkus

Gutmann, Joanna. *The Stress Workbook*, Sheldon Press

Quillam, Susan. *Sensual Pleasures*, Ward Lock

Love, Dr Patricia and Robinson, Jo. *Hot Monogamy*, Piatkus

Litvinoff, Sarah. *The Relate Guide To Sex In Loving Relationships*, Vermilion

Feinmann, Jane. *Surviving The Baby Blues*, Ward Lock

Faber, Adele and Mazlish, Elaine. *How To Talk So Kids Will Listen and Listen So Kids Will Talk*, Avon Books

Hayman, Suzie. *The Relate Guide To Second Families*, Vermilion